Kant's Idealism

Kant's Idealism

by
Philip J. Neujahr

MERCER
• 1995 •

ISBN 0-86554-476-X   MUP/P122

Kant's Idealism
Copyright ©1995
Mercer University Press, Macon, Georgia 31210-3960
All rights reserved
Printed in the United States of America

The paper used in this publication
meets the minimum requirements of American National Standard
for Information Sciences—Permanence of Paper
for Printed Library Materials, ANSI Z39.48-1984.

Library of Congress Cataloging-in-Publication Data

On file with LOC.

Contents

Preface vii

Introduction 1

<u>Chapter 1</u>
Idealism, Transcendental and Otherwise 5
  A. Definition of Idealism 5
  B. Kant's Characterization of Transcendental Idealism 6

<u>Chapter 2</u>
The Status of Kant's Knowing Subject 11
  A. Possible Interpretations of Kant 11
  B. A Look at the Secondary Literature 18
  C. Appealing to the Text 29
    1. Kant's Terminology 29
    2. The Causal Theory of Perception 33
    3. The "I think." Phenomena and Noumena 40
  D. Conclusion. Kant's View of the Knowing Subject.
     The "Empirical Reality" of Space and Time 42

<u>Chapter 3</u>
The Relation of Consciousness to Its Object 45
  A. The Background of Kant's Question 45
  B. Kant's Correspondence Theory of Consciousness 47
  C. Phenomena and Noumena 54
  D. Kant's Coherence Theory of Consciousness 58
    1. Intuitions and Concepts 58
    2. Concepts and Reality 62
    3. The Transcendental Object 64

    4. A Disagreement with Strawson 66
    5. The Concept of External Reality
       and Kant's Coherence Theory 67
  E. Textual Statements of Kant's Coherence Theory 69
    1. Transcendental Deduction, First Edition 69
    2. Transcendental Deduction, Second Edition 75
    3. The Second Analogy of Experience 77
  F. Kant's Use of "Real" in the Text 83
  G. The Relation of Kant's Two Theories
     of Consciousness in the Text 86
  H. The Refutation of Idealism 88

Chapter 4
Summary. Possible Interpretations of Kant's Idealism 95

Chapter 5
The Sources of Kant's Different Idealist Doctrines 101

Chapter 6
"Empirical," "Transcendent," and "Transcendental" 107
  A. A Modest Proposal 107
  B. A Disagreement with Allison 110

Chapter 7
Epilogue. Kant without Idealism? 123

Indexes 131

Preface

This monograph arose, ultimately, out of the difficulties I had as an undergraduate and graduate student in attempting to understand the philosophy of Immanuel Kant. In my initial studies I was especially puzzled over the status that Kant accords the space-time world. While some of my fellow students, and some of our professors, believed that according to Kant this world is in some fairly strong sense "in the mind" of the observing and thinking subject, others argued that for Kant it exists as a spatial and temporal realm quite independent of human persons and independently possesses the material and causal qualities we attribute to it. Both sides in this debate could point to supporting texts in the first *Critique* and to other portions of Kant's philosophy that seemed to uphold their favored interpretation. Kant's own statements that this world is empirically real and transcendentally ideal did not at the time seem to do much to settle the issue.

I attempted to study and think my way through this question during my initial teaching of Kant's philosophy at Oglethorpe University, and I began to develop my own perspective on Kant's use of "real" and its cognates in relation both to the space-time realm and to the thing in itself. I spent a sabbatical year at Princeton University in 1980–1981, during which time, among other projects, I worked on this question further and prepared a very rough draft of the present monograph. Over the next few years I did further research on this topic and gave particular attention to Henry Allison's important book *Kant's Transcendental Idealism*. I spent some further time at Princeton in the fall of 1988. In addition to research I was doing on the philosophy of Leibniz, I thought more about Kantian questions and studied Paul Guyer's recent work, *Kant and the Claims of Knowledge*. Finally, in the spring of 1994 I was given a sabbatical leave to put whatever finishing touches were necessary on my manuscript and to bring it up to date in light of the recent literature on Kant.

Anyone writing about Kant must be struck by the astounding quantity of scholarship on Kant's philosophy that has been produced from Kant's day to the present, some of which is as difficult to read and interpret as Kant's Critical works themselves, and one must feel depressed at the seeming hopelessness of ever coming to terms with more than a small fraction of this literature. In spite of my own efforts to take the most important and most recent of the writings on

Kant into account in my own research, I can by no means be confident that I have not overlooked some monograph or essay—perhaps especially in the most recent literature—that either echoes my own interpretation of Kant or refutes it. This possibility of overlooking relevant works is, I think, one of the inherent anxieties of Kant scholarship. All I can promise the reader is that this monograph represents my best efforts to clarify some difficult and important issues in Kant's philosophy.

I am grateful to Oglethorpe University for giving me the sabbatical leaves I have used to work on his project. I am grateful also to the philosophy department at Princeton University for granting me the status of visiting fellow during 1980–1981 and again in 1988. The generous support I received at Princeton has been crucial to the completion of this work.

Among the many persons who have helped me with my manuscript I am most indebted to Professor Margaret Wilson at Princeton. She advised me during my initial writing of *Kant's Idealism*, read the first draft carefully and made a great many helpful comments on it and criticisms of it, and has continued to monitor my progress on this work with advice and moral support down to the present. I am very grateful to Professor Wilson for the many hours of her valuable time and effort that she has devoted to helping me with my project.

I must also give thanks to Professor Karl Ameriks at the University of Notre Dame for reading an early version of my manuscript and giving me helpful advice on it, and also for giving me suggestions about the most important recent literature on Kant.

The help I received from Margaret Wilson and Karl Ameriks does not, of course, imply that they agree with the interpretation of Kant I have developed.

I would like to give special thanks to two of the secretaries at Oglethorpe University, Gladys Talley and Nora Krebs, and also to a student, Justin Jones, for their efforts in typing and editing my manuscript.

Finally, thanks must go to my colleague and wife Victoria Weiss for her help in reading my work and making her own comments on it. Because of Professor Weiss's literary talents—she is a professor of literature at Oglethorpe—any clarity or writing facility to be found in *Kant's Idealism* is largely due to her.

—*Philip J. Neujahr*

Introduction

One of the more contentious issues in recent scholarship on the philosophy of Immanuel Kant has been the question of whether Kant's transcendental idealism is a good thing or a bad thing. Debate on this question over the last three decades was stimulated by the appearance in 1966 of P. F. Strawson's book, *The Bounds of Sense*. In that work Strawson attempts to detach the "analytic argument" in Kant from the transcendental idealism with which it is unfortunately (in Strawson's view) entwined and to present the resulting purified Kantianism as, among other things, a realist refutation of Cartesian skepticism. Strawson feels that Kant's transcendental idealism and the "imaginary subject" of transcendental psychology in terms of which this idealism is expressed serve only to obscure what is of permanent value in Kant's work. *The Bounds of Sense* has been followed by a succession of works which have attempted in various ways to perform what J. N. Findley has called the transcendental excision upon the Critical philosophy in the hope that, once the tumor of transcendental idealism has been removed, the patient will "bound from the operating table" as something interesting and useful to present-day analytic thought.

Predictably, there has been a reaction against these attempts to liberate Kant from his idealism. Some recent writers on Kant have attempted to explicate and in some cases to defend transcendental idealism against its detractors. The most ambitious attempt along these lines is by Henry Allison in *Kant's Transcendental Idealism*. Allison argues that Kant's version of idealism is a sober and respectable doctrine that, at least "with a bit of help from the sympathetic interpreter," can be presented as a plausible option for philosophers today.[1] Subsequent

---

[1]Henry Allison, *Kant's Transcendental Idealism* (New Haven: Yale University Press, 1983). I deal with Allison's interpretation of Kant in some detail below,

writers on Kant have taken up Allison's attempt to explain transcendental idealism rather than explaining it away, and this interest in the exact nature and status of Kant's idealism shows no sign of exhaustion.[2]

I wish to contribute to this debate by venturing my own explanation of what Kant's transcendental idealism is and how it relates to the rest of his philosophy. I contend that neither those who have attacked transcendental idealism nor those who have defended it have succeeded in their aims. The reason for this, I believe, is that there is no single doctrine that is Kant's transcendental idealism. Rather, Kant's philosophy goes in quite different directions with regard to those questions that determine the nature of any sort of idealism. Furthermore, the conflicting directions in Kant's idealism have important repercussions upon Kant's doctrine of the thing in itself and upon the question of the sort of reality Kant is able to grant to the space-time world. Just as there is no one theory that is Kant's transcendental idealism, so, I argue, there is no single doctrine of the thing in itself and no single view that is conveyed by Kant's claim that the physical world is empirically real and transcendentally ideal.

In my reading of Kant I am clearly in the "negative" camp with interpreters such as Kemp Smith and Strawson, who have argued that the parts of Kant's philosophy do not fit together and hence cannot all be accepted as true. My interpretation is opposed to the "positive" camp of Paton, Allison, and other sympathetic critics who have argued that Kant's philosophy does, at least in its most important doctrines, form a unified whole. In a way, my stance toward Kant is even more critical than that of Kemp Smith and Strawson, for I argue that the conflicts in Kant's thought are serious and deep-seated. Kant's idealism is pushed in different directions by factors that are all quite important to his overall philosophy, and this, I am afraid, bodes ill for the prospect of creating a

---

in chap. 6.

[2] For a good account of the recent interest in transcendental idealism and in Kant's transcendental psychology, see Karl Ameriks's "Kantian Idealism Today" in *History of Philosophy Quarterly* 9 (1992): 329-42. Ameriks argues that on the topic of transcendental idealism, Kant scholarship "has yet to have been overcome by consensus." For a review of previous approaches to Kant, most of which have regarded Kant's idealism as an obstacle rather than an inspiration, see Ameriks's "Recent Work on Kant's Theoretical Philosophy" in *American Philosophical Quarterly* 1 (1982): 1-24.

single, consistent Kantian standpoint by any simple deletion or modification of the elements in Kant's thought.

The organization of this monograph is as follows. In the first chapter I consider the nature of idealism as such and the question of what it can mean to call any philosophy idealistic. I then look at Kant's efforts in the *Critique of Pure Reason* and the *Prolegomena* to make clear his own particular version of idealism, his transcendental idealism (and empirical realism), and to distinguish this view from the transcendental realism (and empirical idealism) of other philosophers. I argue that in spite of his repeated attempts, Kant does not succeed in presenting a single, coherent doctrine under the heading of transcendental idealism.

In my next two chapters I attempt to show why Kant fails to describe a single kind of idealism. There are two questions the answers to which, I contend, determine the nature of any version of idealism. The first has to do with who exactly the idealist's perceiving or knowing "mind" is and how this cognitive subject is supposed to relate to human beings. The second question concerns the relation of this subject to its object. It is the question of how this perceiving and thinking mind "determines" its object in knowing it, and indeed, what it even means to say that the mind's consciousness is "of an object" at all. Kant's differing answers to these questions are what prevent his philosophy from presenting any single idealist view.

In chapter 4 I explore the possible reasons for these differing idealistic directions in Kant's thought. I suggest that Kant's philosophy is pulled in different ways by the tensions between his theory of perception and his theory of thought. In Kant's view of perception (or sensibility) the subject of perception is identified with the individual human person and the object of perception is regarded as existing and having a nature of its own independent of its being perceived. Kant's doctrine of thought (or understanding), on the other hand, pulls his idealism in the opposite direction regarding both the identity of the knowing mind and the relation of this mind to its object.

One of the implications of this theory is that the subject of experience cannot possibly be the individual person but must rather have some status transcending human beings. Furthermore, the object of thought, according to Kant's doctrine of the understanding, is constituted as an actually existing, objectively real thing solely by the activities of the understanding, and there is therefore no room in this view for any nonmental or extramental reality outside of the mind's cognitive activity.

In spite of his efforts to combine them into a single theory of experience, Kant's doctrines of perception and thought do not fit together, and this lack of fit is what ultimately prevents there from being any single Kantian ("transcendental") version of idealism. It is also one of the things that makes Kant's philosophy so difficult.

In my next chapter I consider the ways the terms, "empirical," "transcendent," and "transcendental," function in Kant's philosophy. I examine how Kant uses these terms and also how, I contend, he ought to have used them in describing his idealism. I also discuss the recent commentary by Henry Allison, whose interpretation of the transcendental nature of Kant's idealism differs markedly from my own.

Finally, as a sort of epilogue, I consider the prospects of attempts such as Strawson's to make Kant's philosophy more palatable to present-day analytic thought by removing some or all of the idealist strands in his doctrines. If my reading of Kant is correct, the likelihood of success in such as enterprise is dubious, at least if the resulting "Kantian" philosophy is supposed to bear much resemblance to Kant's own views.

Chapter 1

Idealism, Transcendental and Otherwise

Definition of Idealism

Idealism may be defined as the view that reality or "the world" is a product of the mind, rather than the mind and its consciousness being a product of something nonmental. Stronger and weaker versions of idealism can be distinguished, according to whether or not the nonmental realm is assigned any independent status at all. The most full-blooded forms of idealism such as Neoplatonism and Berkeleyan phenomenalism hold that anything nonmental or extramental has no independent existence or nature of its own at all but is rather entirely a product of the minds, or Mind, or Spirit, which hold it in being. A somewhat weaker doctrine, but still perhaps classifiable as a form of idealism, would be the view that only certain aspects of the world, including its specifically "material" qualities, are mind-imposed. Such a weaker version of idealism would hold that there is a reality existing independent of the mind, to which the mind is somehow related, but that all of the characteristics which denominate something as a material object or material world are mind-imposed and hence characterize this independent reality only as it appears, not as it is itself. The contrast between these stronger and weaker versions of idealism will, of course, be only as clear as the concept of matter or a material object. But if we take spatiality and temporality as necessary conditions of something being material in nature, then a philosopher such as Kant who holds that space and time are "in us" and hence dependent upon the mind will be an idealist in (at least) the weaker sense of this term. It is also clear enough that the philosophy of John Locke should not be classed as idealist at all, because those "primary" qualities of size, shape, density, and so on, which Locke claims to exist independently of the mind, are surely sufficient to make the object which possesses these qualities material in nature.

Something also needs to be said about the nature of the dependence of reality, or its material aspects, upon the mind in idealist theories. If this dependence is not further specified, then standard Christian theism would qualify as a version of idealism. This would give an excessively wide sense to this notion, however, because even though Christian doctrine does hold the material universe to be a creation of God, it in no sense regards this world as being a part of God or within the mind of God. Furthermore, in the theistic view God has created the universe through a decree of His Will rather than by perception or thought. Although it is hard to legislate about such matters, it would perhaps be well to restrict the idealist label to theories which hold that the world, or its material aspects, are dependent upon the specifically cognitive activities of the mind or Mind in perceiving or thinking about (or "experiencing") the object of its awareness.

Kant's Characterization of Transcendental Idealism

With this broad definition of idealism as the view that the "mind" (in some sense) is responsible for at least the "material" aspects of the object of its awareness, we may turn to Kant's attempts to explain his own version of idealism. There are only two places in the *Critique of Pure Reason* where Kant attempts explicitly to distinguish his own form of idealism from the kinds of idealism which are espoused by other philosophers. The first of these passages is in the fourth Paralogism of the Transcendental Dialectic (A367-80), where Kant deals with the problem of how one can be sure of the existence of "outer" objects, things independent of the mind, if one is "directly" conscious only of things within the mind. Kant's treatment of this problem rests upon an unquestioning acceptance of the doctrine that a person can be immediately aware only of the contents of his own mind. Whether these objects of immediate perception be called "ideas" or "perceptions" or "representations," they exist only in being perceived and have only that nature which they are perceived to have. Such a view was part of the philosophical currency of Kant's day and Kant takes it for granted here. Taking this view of immediate awareness, Kant defines a transcendental realist as one who believes that time and space are "things in themselves" and thus that physical objects, in their character as things extended and situated in space and time, exist independent of our awareness of them. But since it is for Kant a fact, presumably accepted by the transcendental realist as well as everyone else, that we can perceive "directly" only our own mental contents, the transcendental realist is then faced with the question of how he can be sure that these other things, material objects outside his mind, exist at all. The transcendental realist thus becomes an empirical idealist, whom Kant defines as one who is in precisely this dilemma. Transcendental realism and empirical idealism are therefore, for Kant, virtually the same doctrine, at least according to this section of the first *Critique*. The transcendental realist regards "representations" and material objects as different sorts of things, and the empirical idealist, accepting this distinction between objects and ideas, simply goes on to ask the obvious question of how we can infer one from the other. The empirical idealist can then become either a skeptical idealist like Descartes, who merely doubts the existence of physical, spatially extended objects, or a dogmatic idealist like Berkeley, who (according to Kant) positively denies the existence of such objects.

The solution to the dilemma of transcendental realism and empirical idealism, Kant tells us, is to be found in transcendental idealism. This is defined by Kant as the doctrine that physical objects, along with the space (and time) in which they are situated, are merely "appearances" and therefore "are to be regarded as being, one and all, representations only, not things in themselves." Having reduced physical objects to representations in the mind, the transcendental idealist is then freed from the perplexity which we find in Descartes and Locke, each of whom is faced with the problem of having to infer one kind of entity from another. The transcendental idealist can therefore be an empirical realist, one who holds that material objects, since they are only representations in the mind, are indeed immediately perceived, and thus that we need not be doubtful about the physical world after all.

Now if this is all that Kant's transcendental idealism amounts to, then it is quite disingenuous for Kant to insist on a sharp contrast between himself and Berkeley. Indeed, the interpretation of Berkeley which Kant puts forward is so wide of the mark that some writers have wondered whether Kant was ignorant of Berkeley's views or whether he deliberately distorted them.[1] Berkeley does deny the existence of matter, under-

---

[1] See especially Colin Turbayne, "Kant's Relation to Berkeley," *Philosophical Quarterly* 5 (1955): 225-44.

stood in a certain philosophically objectionable sense, but he most vehemently affirms the existence of "material," spatial objects such as chairs and stones and trees. Indeed, Berkeley's strategy for responding to the "skeptical idealist" such as Descartes or Locke would seem to be identical with the strategy of Kant: simply define physical objects in terms of mental "representations," say that physical objects are therefore directly perceived after all, and then declare the skeptical problem solved. Therefore Berkeley, as well as Kant, should be considered a transcendental idealist in Kant's sense of this expression.

The other passage in the first *Critique* in which Kant discusses his transcendental idealism occurs later in the Transcendental Dialectic, in section #6 of the Antinomy of Pure Reason (A491-93). What Kant says here is not quite what he says in the fourth Paralogism. In the Antinomy, Kant defines transcendental idealism as the doctrine which he has "sufficiently proved" in the Transcendental Aesthetic, that

> everything intuited in space or time, and therefore all objects of any experience possible to us, are nothing but appearances, that is, mere representations, which, in the manner in which they are represented, as extended beings, or as series of alternations, have no independent existence outside our thoughts.

The transcendental realist is one who "treats these modifications of our sensibility as self-subsistent things." Here the transcendental realist seems to be, for Kant, one who does not recognize any distinction between representations and objects at all, but who thinks that we just "directly" perceive objects which are independent of the mind. Kant's empirical idealist in the Antinomy seems to be one who does distinguish between mental representations and external, physical objects. Kant says that empirical idealism, "while it admits the genuine reality of space, denies the existence of the extended beings in it, or at least considers their existence doubtful." Now under this definition of empirical idealism, it is difficult to see who has ever held such a doctrine. Kant seems to be envisioning someone who believes that a spatial world exists independent of his mind, but who fears that this external world might consist of nothing but empty space. These doubts which the empirical idealist has about material objects must arise, presumably, from his recognition that in his supposed perception of material objects he really "directly" perceives only states of his own mind. At any rate, the proper antidote for this perplexity is to take the transcendental idealist view that "this space and this time [which we perceive], and with them all appearances, are not in themselves *things*; they are nothing but representations, and cannot exist outside our mind."

Thus in the Antinomy, as well as in the fourth Paralogism, Kant's transcendental idealism seems to be much closer to Berkeleyan idealism than Kant wants to admit. In addition, it appears that both Kant and Berkeley, like the "skeptical idealists" from whom they are trying to distance themselves, are committed to some form of inferential argument after all. Berkeley infers from the vividness and order of our perceptual ideas that there must exist a God who puts these ideas into human minds. Kant, on the other hand, believes in a realm of things in themselves, objects independent of our minds, which somehow "affect" our minds to "produce" the sensory data which the mind then puts into a spatial and temporal order. It is questionable how much of an improvement either of these inferences is, over the simpler inference of Locke from ideas to physical objects. If Descartes and Locke have trouble getting outside the mind to physical objects, then Berkeley and Kant should have the same trouble reaching God and things in themselves.

There is reason to think that Kant was not happy with the sort of idealism which was attributed to him upon the initial publication of the *Critique of Pure Reason*. In this first edition of his work, there are the two discussions of the contrast between empirical and transcendental idealism which I have described. In the *Prolegomena to Any Future Metaphysics*, published two years later, Kant complains at some length about the misunderstandings of his theories and says at one point (293-94 in the Academy edition) that he has chosen to retract the expression, "transcendental idealism," and to call his view "critical idealism" instead. In an appendix to the *Prolegomena* (374-75), where he is describing "what sort of idealism it is which goes through my whole work," Kant once again avoids the label of transcendental idealism in favor of calling his theory "'formal' or, better still, 'critical' idealism." In the second edition of the *Critique of Pure Reason*, published four years after the *Prolegomena*, Kant has deleted entirely the fourth Paralogism, which is by far the clearest and most extensive treatment anywhere in his writings of his own transcendental idealism and its contrast with empirical idealism. In those portions of the *Critique of Pure Reason* which were added in the second edition, the expressions, "empirical idealism" and "transcendental idealism" do not occur at all.

All of this suggests rather strongly, I think, that Kant found the terminology of "empirical" versus "transcendental" increasingly unhelpful in explaining his views and that he therefore tended to discard it. It is remarkable, in fact, that commentators on Kant seem to have much more confidence in these labels than Kant himself had. But in spite of his indecision over what expressions to use, Kant seems to be convinced that his problems are only terminological. He is quite confident that there is a distinctive form of Kantian idealism which differs from the kinds of idealism and realism espoused by his philosophical predecessors and contemporaries, and that his difficulty is only in finding the proper label to apply to this doctrine.

Unfortunately, Kant's own problems here are more than just terminological. To see why, we must consider the Kantian answers to two questions, "Who is the subject of experience?" and "What is the mind's relation to its object?" Let us consider first the status of the Kantian "mind" or subject of experience.

Chapter 2

The Status of Kant's Knowing Subject

Possible Interpretations of Kant

The natural assumption that one makes, upon an initial reading of the first *Critique* or the *Prolegomena*, is that Kant's cognitively active subject of experience, which imposes its own innate form upon the matter of experience, is simply the individual human person. What are the implications of interpreting Kant in this way? First of all, it is misleading to speak of the Kantian subject as literally putting the given "matter" of sensation into space and time, or as having space and time (and substance, causation, etc.) "in the mind." It is more accurate, although more cumbersome, to say that according to Kant the subject of experience possesses certain faculties which operate in such a way that the object of consciousness appears to the subject *as* a universe of things which are, as individual items, extended and related to one another in space and time and which possess a number of additional characteristics that presuppose (at least) existence in time; but that all of the spatial and temporal facts about the perceived world characterize the object of awareness only as it appears to the knowing mind.

Now if the subject here is the individual person, then this event of "the object appearing to the subject" will occur in many instances as there are persons. Viewing Kant in this way will lead us to deny that there is, for Kant, a single, public space and time, indeed any sort of unified world at all. This Kantian picture will give us "the object" plus a plurality of individual minds, each of which will bear a strong resemblance to a Leibnizian monad. For if the object appears to each subject, in a separate cognitive event, as a space-time world, what relation will these individual persons, these subjects of experience, have to one another? They can have no spatial relation because space is merely a way in which the object appears to each subject because of the subject's own mental faculties. Likewise, one cannot say that these subjects exist at the same time, or before or after one another, since there is no single time which includes them all. There is no single time because temporal duration (and temporal relation) is only one of the ways in which the object appears to each individual subject and does not characterize either object or subject in itself.

The similarity of Kant's view of the knowing subject, as so interpreted, to that of Leibniz is obvious. According to Leibniz the world consists of an infinity of monads, each of which is regarded as a simple spiritual substance on the model of a Cartesian ego. Space and time in this view are "phenomena bene fundata." The interpretation of Leibniz is, of course, a risky business, especially regarding the nature of space, on which Leibniz seems to have had two different doctrines.[1] One of these doctrines claims that space either is, or is at least derived from or "grounded in," the real relation that monads have to one another. In Leibniz's more esoteric (and consistent) view, the monads have no real relation to one another at all. This is what make them monads, and it is the absence of relational properties which is expressed in Leibniz's picturesque statement that these ultimate substances have no windows. Here space is not a real property of any kind, either monadic or relational, but is rather one of the ways in which the totality of monads appears to, or is reflected in, each individual monad due to the cognitive faculties of the monad. Although Leibniz is even less clear and explicit about time than about space, the esoteric Leibniz would presumably tell a similar story to the effect that since monads have no real relation to one another at all, time can be only a way in which things appear to each separate monad.

If the Kantian subject is taken to be the individual person, such that there are many of these ultimate subjects each of whom has his own space and time in the sense described, then the Kantian philosophy will indeed have a Leibnizian look about it. There will exist a multitude of separate centers of consciousness (plus "the object," whose relation to these minds has yet to be discussed), but there will be no single space

---

[1] See Norman Kemp Smith, *A Commentary to Kant's "Critique of Pure Reason,"* 2nd ed. (Atlantic Highlands NJ: Humanities Press, 1923) 298-99.

and time and hence no public world in which these individual minds can exist and interact with one another.

Is there anything wrong with this as an interpretation of Kant? It certainly fits one's initial impression upon reading Kant's Critical writings, given the psychological terminology which Kant uses in stating his Copernican Revolution (see below, 29-30). Furthermore, since Kant's philosophical upbringing involved heavy exposure to the views of Leibniz, it should be not be surprising if Kant's own philosophy should be Leibnizian in some respects. Yet a little thought will show that this monadistic interpretation of Kant simply will not do. It cannot possibly do justice to all of Kant's intentions in his philosophy. Kant says that "the subject" imposes the most basic features of the physical world, but does he mean the subject as it appears, or as it is in its own intrinsic nature? Surely the latter. It can be only the subject as it is in itself which passively receives sensory data, which possesses the faculties of sense and thought, and which, by means of these faculties, experiences what it is aware of in the ways explored by Kant in the first *Critique*. But this subject, the subject as it is in itself, cannot be the individual person. For one thing, the individual person, the particular human being, is a material object in space and time who interacts causally with other things; and none of these features can in Kant's view characterize anything as it is in itself. Consider further the distinction between two different persons, you and me, for instance. Each of us is *one* person, we are *different from* one another, and together we constitute a *plurality* of persons. But these features as well, according to Kant, have their origin in the mind of the subject and can therefore characterize something only as it appears, not as it is in itself. Kant holds that space, time, and the categories do *not* apply to the thing in itself and hence not to the subject of experience in its own intrinsic nature,[2] and this fact would prevent Kant from saying that subjects in themselves are identical with human beings or even that they are correlated one-to-one with them. Whether or not an attribution of such concepts as unity and plurality to the subject in itself is even meaningful in Kant's view, it is certainly incorrect; and if Kant felt that he could not legitimately assert a multitude of separate subjects in themselves, then he could not have taken a monadological interpretation of his own philosophy.

---

[2] For a defense of this interpretation of Kant, see below, chap. 3.

Suppose we say that the Kantian subject which is the source of space, time, causation, etc., is not the individual person but some other subject of experience. Such a view would seem to offer the best hope for getting a single space-time world out of the Kantian philosophy. If this ultimate subject is in some sense different from us human persons and is something of which there is not a plurality of instances, then perhaps we could tell the following story. We could say that "the object" appears to "the subject" as a single universe of things in space and time. Within this physical universe which is the object-as-it-appears there are individual sentient beings, each of whom perceives and thinks about things in its environment by means of its individual cognitive faculties. We could then go on, if we wished, to describe this physical world in terms of the scientific realism of Kant's day. We could adopt a causal theory of perception and speak of individual persons perceiving material objects by causal interaction through the sense organs. If we found John Locke's account persuasive, we could adopt his view of primary and secondary qualities and could draw a distinction between reality and appearance within this physical world. According to such an account, human beings do not perceive physical objects exactly as they are in themselves. Not only do things have many properties which we are not presently aware of but which we may, perhaps, discover in the progress of science, but in addition our own sensory apparatus makes objects appear to us as having properties such as color, sound, and smell, which these objects do not possess in their own intrinsic natures. To keep this entire story Kantian, we would have to remind ourselves that everything described in this account, including the difference within this world between how material things appear to human beings and how they are in themselves, pertains only to appearance; it is all within the appearance of "the object" to "the subject." Using Kantian terminology, all of these distinctions within the space-time world would be given the label of "empirical." Calling the entire physical world (in a "transcendental" sense) appearance, we would then speak of the empirical distinction, relative to human beings, between appearance and reality and of empirical subjects as the persons making this distinction. Any mental operations performed by individual humans would likewise be labeled empirical, whether or not they were analogous to the functions of synthesis performed upon a sensory manifold which Kant describes in the first *Critique*. For the account in the *Critique of Pure Reason*, although presented in a psychological idiom, constitutes transcendental psychology. It is a description of the activities of "the subject" in being aware of "the object," and it is these transcendental activities which *produce* the physical world which contains individual persons. An advocate of this interpretation would insist that the (logically) initial affection of the thing in itself upon the subject is not to be confused with the (logically) subsequent affection of empirical objects upon empirical selves. The first is a timeless relation which produces the physical world—a relation between two unknown and, to us, unknowable entities. The second is a relation within this world which involves the temporal sequence of cause and effect.

This view of the Kantian subject resembles somewhat the double affection interpretation of Kant which was developed by Erich Adickes.[3] One difficulty with this interpretation is that it makes it quite impossible to specify any relation between the cognitive "subject" of the first *Critique* and individual persons. Although Adickes himself wishes to declare that the two subjects are the same even though their transcendental and empirical "affections" are different, it is hard to see how such an identification could be made intelligible. For human beings, as objects of external awareness and internal introspection, exist in space and time and hence are, for Kant, part of the phenomenal world. They, along with everything else in space-time reality, constitute "the object" as it appears to the form-imposing cognitive subject. As parts of the phenomenal universe, therefore, human beings would seem to have no closer connection to the cognitive mind of Kant's first *Critique* than any other object in the phenomenal universe.

This lack of any specifiable connection between human beings and the Kantian subject of experience would seem to constitute a fatal flaw in the double affection interpretation of Kant, at least in terms of certain of the aims of Kant's philosophy. Two of Kant's major motives in instituting his Copernican Revolution were to account for our a priori knowledge and to solve what Kant calls the Antinomies. Regarding knowledge, Kant is puzzled by the fact that we can know a priori that certain facts must be true of the world of our experience, the world of things in space and time. This puzzle is solved by declaring that "we ourselves" are the source of these a priori knowable aspects of the universe. We have only to look within ourselves, Kant says, and we can

---

[3] Erich Adickes, *Kant's Lehre von der Deppelten Affection Unseres Ich* (Tübingen: J. C. B. Mohr Verlag, 1929).

discern what the mind contributes to experience, and hence we can know prior to experience how the object of our awareness must appear to us. But for this strategy to work, the form-imposing subject must be the same subject as the one who possesses a priori knowledge about the physical world. Only if I impose sensible and conceptual form upon the sensory data of my experience, and you do the same for yours, and Kant does the same for his, can each of us know a priori how his or her experience must be. If, on the other hand, the form-imposing subject is not you or I and has no specifiable relation to your mind or to mine, then how should the cognitive activities of this subject have any relevance to what you or I can know a priori about the physical world?

Of the Antinomies of Reason in the Transcendental Dialectic portion of the first *Critique*, it is the first and third which are the most relevant to our question of how the Kantian subject relates to individual human beings. In the third Antinomy Kant asks whether everything in the world is causally determined or if there is a place for human freedom. Kant uses his distinction between mind-structured appearance and thing in itself to declare that a person as object of our experience must be causally determined in every detail but that this same person considered as he is in himself is, or may be, free. There are some difficulties regarding the conception of freedom which Kant is working with here, but the crucial point for us is this: Kant is distinguishing in the third Antinomy between a person as appearance and this same subject in his own intrinsic nature. It is this underlying subject in itself which imposes the moral law and which also possesses the freedom either to follow it or not. It is therefore not open to Kant or his interpreters to say that the Kantian subject in itself has no particular relation to human beings. If the application of praise and blame, reward and punishment, to individual human beings is to make any sense, as Kant clearly wishes it to, it seems that the physical person and the subject in itself must be correlated at least to the extent that there is one such subject for each physical person. If I am to be punished for my wickedness and you are to be rewarded for your virtue, then surely Kant must say that I as I am in myself freely chose evil and that you as you are in yourself freely chose to do right. Otherwise, why would it make any sense to do one thing to my physical person and something else to yours? All of this would seem to imply that I "in myself" and you "in yourself" are at least two *different* agents, and thus that there is one morally free agent per human being. The obvious question at this point is whether the moral self, which imposes the moral law through the autonomy of its will, is the same self as the cognitive self which imposes sensible and conceptual form upon its experience. There is nothing in Kant's writings to suggest that he wished to separate the two, and indeed it is difficult to see how he could, since it is one and the same physical person who feels constrained by the moral law and possesses a priori knowledge about the physical world. So it must be this person *in himself* who engages in both moral and epistemic law making, and thus there must be as many of these epistemic subjects as there are human persons.

The first Antinomy, likewise, seems to require one subject in itself per person. This Antinomy has to do with the spatial and temporal extent of the universe and consists of a set of opposing arguments which show both that the universe must have had a beginning in time and must be finite in spatial extent, and also that it could not have had a beginning and must be spatially infinite. Kant says that if space and time were things in themselves this problem would be insoluble, since both sets of arguments are valid under this assumption. But because space and time are only forms of sensibility and the physical universe as a result is only the product of the subject's awareness, we can render the Antinomy harmless by declaring both conclusions false. The physical universe *in itself* is neither finite nor infinite because it is not anything *in itself* at all. We may say that this universe is potentially indefinitely large in space and time, but this is only to say the subject of experience as his knowledge advances will be able to continue his historical researches back into the past and his spatial explorations out from where he now is, without ever reaching a boundary in either case. The subject imposes space and time upon the object of his experience, and so, this being the origin of space and time, there is no possibility that the subject will ever come to the end of either of them.

If the subject of experience here is something which there is one of per individual person, such that I impose space and time on my experience and you impose them on yours, then Kant's strategy in the first Antinomy seems at least promising. I individually could never reach the boundary of the universe, nor must I say that the universe already exists as something actually infinite, since I myself am the source of the spatial (and temporal) extent of the universe which I am exploring. But now let us suppose that the imposer of space and time is a subject which has no special relation to human beings. In this case space and time will exist quite independently of you and me as individual persons, and independently even of the human race as a whole. We can put the label of "appearance" upon this entire universe, but this will not alter the fact that in relation to human beings this space-time order is something existing in its own right. On this interpretation of the Kantian subject, any space which I discover already existed prior to my discovery of it. I can, therefore, perfectly well ask how much space actually exists now waiting for me to explore it, an infinite quantity or only a limited amount, and I can formulate an analogous question about time. These questions would perhaps be equivalent to a question about what spatial and temporal extent "the subject" encompasses within its consciousness, just as one can ask about the extent of the perceptual field of a human being.

Merely calling the space-time world "appearance" does not, therefore, prevent us from asking whether this world has a certain (finite) size or is infinitely large. This will be a perfectly reasonable question if the subject which is the source of space and time is not the individual you or I, and if the physical would which you and I live in exists independently of us. All of this indicates that the Kantian subject of experience must somehow be the individual person; only some very close connection between the form-imposing subject and human beings will enable Kant's arguments in the Antinomies to achieve their intended result. It seems, therefore, that the arguments of the Antinomies must push us back toward our original monadistic interpretation of the Kantian subject.

A Look at the Secondary Literature

Both of these interpretations of the subject of experience thus present grave difficulties for Kant's philosophy. So what are we to say about the Kantian subject? A look at the literature on Kant[4] is disconcerting because we find interpreters of Kant taking confident but opposing positions on this question. Erich Adickes adopts the double affection view of Kant described above (14-15), according to which the "affection" of object upon subject which produces the space-time world is to be sharply distinguished from the causal "affection" of material objects upon human beings. Rather than adopting a corollary distinction between the two

---

[4]*Some* of the literature on Kant's Critical philosophy; or to be more exact, a few of the best-known commentators on Kant written (mostly) in English in the twentieth century.

kinds of subject of experience, however, Adickes declares that they are identical:

> Ebenso sind Ich an sich und empirisches Ich nicht zwei verschiedene Subjecte. Sondern ein und dasselbe Ich ist einmal an und fur sich zeitlos und darum unerkennbar, anderseits wird es in meinem empirischen Bewusstsein in der Form der Zeit, also erscheinungsweise, von mir, d.h. von ihm selbst, erlebt und erkannt.[5]
> (Yet the I in itself and the empirical I are not two distinct subjects. Rather one and the same I is, in and of itself, timeless and therefore unknowable, but it also becomes experienced and known in my empirical consciousness by me, i.e., by itself, under the form of time, thus as appearance.)

Merely stating this identity, however, does not render it intelligible. In fairness to Adickes, though, it should be noted that he died before completing *Kant's Lehre von der Doppelten Affection Unseres Ich* (*Kant's Doctrine of the Double Affection of Our "I"*). The last chapter of this work was to have been titled, "Die Schwierigkeiten, in die die Lehre der doppelten Affection fuhrt" ("The difficulties, into which the doctrine of double affection leads"). In this final chapter Adickes might have dealt with the problems of relating Kant's form-imposing subject to individual persons.

Of the writers in English, Norman Kemp Smith adopts something like Adickes' view of double affection, holding that for Kant human sensory awareness is a causal, empirical affection which takes place within the space-time world, a world which is the result of another affection, that between "the subject" and "the object." Unlike Adickes, however, Kemp Smith is quite willing to allow for a total bifurcation of the form-imposing Kantian subject and individual human beings. To more precise, he recognizes two distinct tendencies of thought in Kant. There is what he calls Kant's subjectivism and his phenomenalism. Kemp Smith regards these as equally genuine components of the first *Critique* but holds that they are of unequal philosophical merit. When Kant is holding to his subjectivism, according to Kemp Smith, he takes the form-imposing subject to be the individual self. "Representations" are then states of mind of these particular persons, and the space-time world is nothing over and above the sum of human conscious states. Kant's whole system then bears some resemblance to that of Berkeley except that instead of

---

[5]Adickes, *Kant's Lehre*, 3.

God causing ideas in the minds of individual subjects (and because of His all-powerful goodness producing them in a certain predictable, coherent manner), there is the thing in itself (or better, just "the object") which is apprehended by whatever subjects there are through their being affected by it. The experiences of these subjects occur in a certain regular manner, not because of God's goodness, but rather as a result of those mental faculties and functions which are necessary conditions of experience, or at least of "our" experience, and which are contained within each individual subject.

This "subjectivist" doctrine in Kant is regard by Kemp Smith as a vestige of previous philosophical systems such as that of Descartes and is given the appellation of pre-Critical or semi-Critical. In contrast to this Kemp Smith places Kant's "phenomenalism" which, he says, is alone fully Critical. According to this view, "our mental states are themselves part of the natural order which consciousness reveals."[6] Human bodies plus all of the other material objects in the universe exist quite independently of the conscious states of human beings. The experiences of a particular human being contribute toward making up that particular empirical self, which shares a common world with other empirical selves. All of these individual selves, or persons, along with everything else in the space-time universe, form a single system of nature. But then this entire system is "conditioned by an underlying realm of noumenal existence."[7] Kemp Smith says that Kant's truly Critical move was to say that those mental processes which generate experience are not consciously apprehended ideas of any kind and do not originate in the individual self. Rather, this cognitive activity generates individual selves plus everything else. Kemp Smith is quite explicit in arguing that according to this most profound, Critical strain in Kant's philosophy, the "given" manifold which is synthesized by the understanding has no special connection with the sensations which are caused in human beings by physical objects acting upon the sense organs. He tells us that the Critical Kant is "culpably careless" in failing to distinguish these two very different meanings of the phrase, "given manifold."[8] Furthermore, the activities of the understanding which Kant describes in the Transcendental Analytic have no

---

[6]Kemp Smith, *Commentary*, xlvi.
[7]Ibid., xlvii.
[8]Ibid., 276.

connection at all with whatever the mind or brain of a human being may do in structuring the experience of that human being. The functions of the human mind are the proper study of empirical psychology, which is quite unrelated to what Kant is dealing with in the first *Critique*.

An obvious question about this interpretation has to do with Kant's use of psychological terms. If those processes which generate the space-time world have no special relation to anything occurring in or to human beings, why does Kant use psychological terminology to describe them? He may be doing transcendental rather than empirical psychology, but if it is to be called psychology of any kind, surely what is describing must have some similarity to human processes. To this question, Kemp Smith gives no clear answer. He does not seem to believe that this properly Critical strand of Kant's thought entails any notion of a cosmic Mind thinking the universe into existence. He says rather that those "synthetic processes" which Kant has proven to "condition all experience" should properly be ascribed to "noumenal conditions which fall outside the realm of possible definition." He admits that we cannot even be certain that these processes of synthesis "may legitimately be described as mental," and says rather that, "We have, indeed, to conceive them on the analogy of our mental processes, but that may only be because of the limitation of our knowledge to the data of our experience." Shortly after this, Kemp Smith says that although the processes or activities which give rise to the space-time universe "may by analogy be described as consisting of synthetic processes acting upon a given material, they are in their real nature unknown to us. Even their bare possibility we cannot profess to comprehend." Why then posit such processes at all, if we manifestly do not know what we are positing? Kemp Smith's only answer to this is the suggestion that "given experience is demonstrably not self-explanatory, and would seem to refer us for explanation to some such antecedent generative grounds."[9]

Another commentator who has no use for the Kantian subject as individual person is George Schrader.[10] Inquiring about the sort of reality which Kant attributes to the physical world, Schrader tells us that "There is no doctrine in [Kant's] philosophy which is more difficult to under-

---

[9]Ibid., 277-78.

[10]George Schrader, "The Transcendental Ideality and Empirical Reality of Kant's Space and Time," *The Review of Metaphysics* 4 (1951): 507-36.

stand" than Kant's assertion that space and time are empirically real and transcendentally ideal. This difficulty stems from the fact that "it is very difficult to see precisely what sort of idealism is supported by the *Critique*."[11] This difficulty, in turn, Schrader says, rests upon the uncertain status of the Kantian subject of experience. Schrader does admit that, according to Kant, "Whatever elements in experience are necessary must be mind-contributed and, hence, ideal," but in asking what Kant means by "mind-contributed," Schrader assures us that according to the most profound, "Critical" side of Kant's thought, "Whatever else may be said about the mind which contributes necessity to experience, it is not the individual knowing subject." He admits that "a good deal of Kant's language is strongly suggestive of a Cartesian point of view," but he agrees with Kemp Smith that those parts of the *Critique* in which the Kantian subject appears to be the individual person do not represent Kant's "critical or transcendental position, which is central to the *Critique*." So then what sort of subject is it which, according to this truly Critical Kantian view, is responsible for the phenomenal world? Schrader feels that "the sort of mind which is capable of imposing an intelligible framework upon appearances must have some sort of cosmic status," and that therefore the post-Kantian Idealists such as Hegel were closer to the spirit of Kant's philosophy than are those present day interpreters who "would read Kant through the eyes of Descartes or Locke."[12]

Turning to the other interpretive camp, one can find commentators who are equally assured that Kant had no intention whatever of making his form-imposing subject anything other than the individual person. One such commentator is H.J. Paton, who speaks throughout his commentary of the human mind as the object of Kant's study in the first *Critique*, and of sensibility, understanding, and all the rest as being human faculties. It is not surprising, therefore, that Paton arrives at the sort of Leibnizian interpretation of Kant which was described earlier. He tells us that it is "not unreasonable to suppose that Kant, under the influence of Leibniz, continued to regard reality as composed of monads."[13] As individual selves I am one monad and you are another. Paton says that these

---

[11]Ibid., 515-16.
[12]Ibid., 533-35.
[13]H. J. Paton, *Kant's Metaphysics of Experience* (New York: MacMillan, 1936) 1:183.

Kantian monads are not windowless, however. Each of us looks out on—is affected by—"the object," which because of our own cognitive faculties appears to each of us as a space-time world. Taking this interpretation of Kant, Paton accordingly worries about how Kant can allow for a single, public space and time which includes all of our individual minds.

In this connection it is interesting to draw a comparison between the philosophy of George Berkeley and that of Kant as interpreted by Paton. When Berkeley speaks of the mind, and of physical objects as being collections of ideas in the mind, he intends to speak only of individual, finite spirits. He does believe in God, of course, but he insists that we are in no way part of the mind of God, nor do we see into the mind of God when we apprehend our own ideas. Berkeley wants to believe in a single, public world, and he wishes to use the notion of God's omniscience as a means to this end, saying that God perceives everything all of the time and hence holds the created universe in existence. But if I am one spirit and you are another and God is yet another, and if each of us perceives only his own individual ideas, it is difficult to see how the fact that God can have more ideas than we can will contribute at all toward making a single, public world. It is to Berkeley's credit that he is willing to ask himself the hard questions here. In the third of his *Dialogues Between Hylas and Philonous,* where most of the embarrassing points are raised, Philonous assures Hylas that the things which I perceive "have an existence exterior to my mind, since I find them by experience to be independent of it." And since it has been shown that the *esse* of physical objects is *percipi*, the fact that the objects which we perceive exist independently of my and your perception of them shows that "there is therefore some other mind wherein they exist, during the intervals between the times of my perceiving them: as likewise they did before my birth, and would do after my supposed annihilation."[14]

Later in this third *Dialogue*, Hylas asks the question which strikes at the heart of Berkeley's attempt at a public world: "But the same idea which is in my mind cannot be in yours, or in any other mind. Doth it not therefore follow, from your principles, that no two can see the same

---

[14] George Berkeley, *Three Dialogues between Hylas and Philonous*, in *The Works of George Berkeley*, ed. A. A. Luce and T. E. Jessop (Edinburgh: Thomas Nelson and Sons, 1948–1957) 230-31.

things? And is not this highly absurd?"[15] What follows from Philonous is a lengthy quibble over the word, "same," which need not be reproduced here. There is some irritation evident in Philonous (or Berkeley) in this passage as he tries to blur the distinction between "same" and "similar" so as to protect himself from this damaging criticism. He clearly fails in this attempt, and the conclusion of it all is that no two spirits ever do literally perceive the same thing. The most that can be said is that they "agree in their perceptions," which means that the ideas which I have in my mind cohere with the ideas in your mind due to the omnipotence and goodness of God. The whole Berkeleyan picture thus bears some resemblance to Leibniz's preestablished harmony, except that for Berkeley the harmony between my ideas and yours is not preestablished but rather requires the continuous activity of God.

Turning back to Paton's interpretation of Kant, we find the same sort of exasperation (and even the quibbling over the meaning of "same") that we find in Berkeley's attempt to secure a public world. Paton, who must be classed as a sympathetic interpreter of Kant, wishes to present a view of Kant's philosophy which present day readers can accept as, in the main, a true account of human knowledge; and so he wants to do justice to our ordinary view that there is a single space and time in which we all live. But since the subject of experience which Paton sees in Kant's writings is as much an individual self as the "mind" in Berkeley, this is not easy:

> It may also be asked how we can know that the same space and time exist for different minds. Even if we assume that each mind comes to reality with similar forms of sensibility, would not this imply that each mind was aware of appearance in a similar, but different, space and time?
>
> This question Kant, so far as I know, has not raised. For my own part I find it difficult to understand what could be meant by saying that each of two men was aware of an infinite and homogenous space (or time), but that nevertheless the spaces (or times) were different. I should have thought that here, if anywhere, the principle of the Identity of Indiscernibles was valid.[16]

In other words, if each of us apprehends "the object" as being a world of things in space and time, and if each of us apprehends it similarly in this

---

[15]Ibid., 247.
[16]Paton, *Kant's Metaphysics*, 1:180.

respect, let us not split hairs over whether there is literally the same space and time for all of us.

It must be said, however, that Paton does not leave the matter here, but returns to the question of the unity of the phenomenal world elsewhere in his commentary. He admits that he finds no attempt by Kant anywhere in the *Critique* to answer the objection that if the phenomenal world exists only relative to the subject and if there are many subjects, then there must be many phenomenal worlds. Paton entertains the idea of interpreting the one phenomenal world, to which Kant seems committed at various places in the *Critique*, as some sort of never-to-be-completed ideal of human experience, expressing both the unlimited extendability of my experience and the fact that my experience and yours are similar in certain a priori knowable ways. Paton does acknowledge, though, that "it seems difficult to me to give a confident answer to this question," and he finally says that this problem of how we can have a common phenomenal world if both the form and matter of experience are "in" the individual human mind is "the central difficulty" of Kant's doctrine as a whole.[17]

Another commentator who should mentioned in this regard is P.F. Strawson, who takes the Kantian subject as being, in Kant's intentions, the individual person, but who sees even better than Paton does the difficulties involved in this. Strawson, like Paton, interprets Kant as holding a monadistic view with space and time being "in" each individual subject and with no single, common space and time relating these centers of consciousness to one another. For Strawson tells us that Kant conceived of his project in the first *Critique* as being primarily "an investigation into the structure and workings of the cognitive capacities of beings such as ourselves."[18] Taking the subject as individual knower, Strawson is then properly dubious about Kant's doctrine that the physical world is empirically real. Kant claims that the empirical idealist takes as certainly real the states of consciousness of individual subjects (or at least of the that subject which is "I" myself), and calls into question the

---

[17]Ibid., 585.

[18]P. F. Strawson, *The Bounds of Sense* (London: Methuen & Co., 1966) 19. This book contains the best treatment of the Kantian subject of experience and the relation of this subject to human beings which I have found in the recent literature on Kant.

existence of any material world distinct from these states of consciousness. The transcendental idealist, however, is an empirical realist and accords "no superiority of status" to states of consciousness over material objects. Strawson recognizes that Kant, at least at certain places in the *Critique*, very much wants to accept the scientific realism of his day. He wants to say that objects in the space-time world, at least in their "primary" qualities, exist completely independently of my experiences or anyone else's. In his Refutation of Idealism in the second edition of the *Critique*, this seems to be the conclusion of his argument. But Strawson argues that regardless of Kant's intentions there is not in fact an "equal reality," in the Kantian philosophy, between bodies in space and states of consciousness in individual minds. For Kant holds that experience arises when "the object" as it is in itself "affects" each of us individual subjects to produce states of consciousness. This affecting relation does not produce states of consciousness *plus* physical objects in space and time. Rather, according to Strawson's interpretation, "*all* the actual effects of these transactions . . . are temporally ordered states of consciousness; but these include . . . and *must* include . . . states of consciousness that we rate as perceptions of bodies of space."[19]

Strawson realizes that Kant cannot simply equate his form-imposing subject with individual human beings because the subject in itself is not in space or time and is not substantial, causal, etc. He also recognizes that Kant cannot even say that the affecting object and the affected subject are, in their own inherent natures, two different things.[20] Yet Strawson sees more clearly than other commentators these two points: first, that if Kant is to accomplish some of the major aims of his philosophy, those of making a place for moral freedom and responsibility, explaining a priori knowledge, and solving the puzzles about space and time in the Antinomies, he needs to establish, in Strawson's strange phrase, some "point of contact, in the way of identity" between the Kantian subject and human persons; second, given that the subject in itself has *none* of the characteristics of a human person, there is nothing intelligible which Kant can possibly say about the connection between "the subject" and you and me. Kant attempts to ignore this difficulty by a free and easy use of personal pronouns, declaring that "we" impose

---

[19]Ibid., 56.
[20]Ibid., 236.

space and time and that "we" are responsible for the order and connection of appearances. As Strawson points out, "the mere use of the personal pronouns and possessives does nothing, however, to show where the point of connection lies."[21]

In any case, Strawson sees Kant as committed in his philosophy to some very close relation here, and so he has no use for an interpretation like that of Kemp Smith. Commenting on the possibility that the "transcendental subject's being affected by things in themselves" generates individual, conscious persons *plus* material objects in space and time, Strawson remarks, "It seems almost too obvious for argument that this is not [Kant's] view." Such a thesis would not even appear to solve the philosophical problems mentioned above, and it would give rise to additional difficulties of its own. If we accepted individual states of consciousness, physical objects, and the thing in itself as three distinct orders of things, then if we said that our perceptions of physical objects were generated by the action upon us of things in themselves, this would require a preestablished harmony to explain our perceptions giving us knowledge of physical objects. On the other hand, if we said that our perceptions were caused by the physical objects themselves, this view "would require us to have real knowledge of the causes of our perceptions, a thesis which Kant also explicitly rejects."[22]

Many commentators on Kant do not enter at all into this question of the relation of the creative "subject" to human beings. In a recent commentary by Ralph C. S. Walker, we are told that Kant rejects the possibility of a "purely sense-datum experience" and argues that the subject of experience must be aware of objects which have an existence independent of the subject's perception of them:

> Independent, that is, in the ordinary sense in which we take physical objects to be independent of us; not in the other, transcendental, sense in which only things in themselves are properly independent of the minds whose synthesis creates the world of appearances.[23]

The question that cries out (in vain) for attention here, is that of the relation between the "us" of which physical objects are taken to be independent, and the "minds" whose activities create these objects.

---

[21]Ibid., 247.
[22]Ibid., 263.
[23]Ralph C. S. Walker, *Kant* (London: Routledge & Kegan Paul, 1978) 111.

The puzzlement over how to interpret Kant's knowing mind has persisted to the present day. In a very recent book, *Kant's Transcendental Psychology*,[24] Patricia Kitcher attempts to rehabilitate and defend the psychological doctrines of Kant's philosophy against detractors such as P.F. Strawson and Jonathan Bennett. In this rehabilitative effort Kitcher regards transcendental psychology not as a story about the timeless activities of a noumenal mind or Mind standing behind the space-time world, but rather as an enormously abstract and schematic account of the activities of the human mind in structuring its experience. It is an account which Kitcher believes should be useful in suggesting directions of inquiry for today's empirical science of cognitive psychology. There is a price to be paid, however, for Kitcher's identification of Kant's knowing subject with the individual human person. This identification can be made, as Kitcher herself acknowledges, only by jettisoning altogether Kant's view that time and space, and the schematized categories, are imposed upon experience by the mind and hence do not characterize the object or subject of experience as they are in themselves.

Kitcher recognizes that if one accepts Kant's transcendental idealism and interprets it as Kant intended, then the mental activities which Kant describes must be interpreted atemporally, which Kitcher, here agreeing with Strawson, says requires "traversing the limits of intelligibility." So in order to salvage Kant's transcendental psychology, she rejects the most distinctive tenet of Kant's idealism. She claims that this move leaves some remnant of transcendental idealism, but in its emasculated form this idealism amounts only to the doctrine that "our knowledge is influenced by the structure of our minds." Kitcher is clear that this reading of Kant does not represent Kant's own intentions, but claims that this "drastic move" is necessary if one is to save the most valuable and interesting part of Kant's philosophy.

Patricia Kitcher's strategy is not open to me, of course, because in this essay I am trying to ascertain just what Kant's transcendental idealism is and how it relates to the rest of his philosophy. What I must do, therefore, in this part of my essay, is to take Kant's idealism in the way, or ways, in which it seems to go in the Kantian texts and then try to see

---

[24]Patricia Kitcher, *Kant's Transcendental Psychology* (New York: Oxford University Press, 1993): see 139-41.

what Kant himself must have believed about the identity of his form-imposing subject.

Appealing to the Text

Kant's Terminology

With the sort of disagreement which we have seen among the commentators about what Kant "obviously" meant to say, at least in the "truly Critical" part of his philosophy, it seems unlikely that we can simply turn to the text of the first *Critique* to settle this question. If we go through the *Critique of Pure Reason* and the *Prolegomena* carefully in search of passages which bear on this problem of the status of the Kantian subject, what we find is disappointing. First of all, there is no doubt that the terminology of the first *Critique* is psychological throughout. In the Preface to the first edition Kant tells us that in his enquiry he is concerned with "nothing save reason itself in its pure thinking," and that knowledge of this is surely attainable because he comes upon this "in my own self" (Axiv). In his initial statement of his Copernican Revolution, Kant says that it is the principle of "our new method of thought . . . that we can know a priori of things only what we ourselves put into them" (Bxviii). There are literally dozens of references throughout the first *Critique* and the *Prolegomena* to space and time as being "in us," of time as being "our mode of inwardly intuiting ourselves" (A34), to the pure concepts as having their "first seeds and dispositions in the human understanding" (A66), and so on. In some passages such as this latter one, Kant uses adjectives such as "human" (*menschlich*) in referring to the mind-imposed form and the faculties which are responsible for it. More commonly, he simply uses pronouns, usually the first person plural but occasionally the pronouns "I" and "you." When he does use the plural personal pronoun, however, he always uses the singular term for the mind and its faculties. Thus he speaks of "our" mind and of "our" sensibility and understanding. Even in this choice of terminology, we see Kant sliding around the question of whether or not there is a separate form-imposing faculty for each one of "us."

In any case, the way in which Kant expresses his Copernican Revolution throughout the *Critique* indicates very strongly that it is Kant himself, plus his readers, plus the rest of humanity, who (individually or collectively) impose space, time and the categories upon what is given in experience. There are even introspective sounding passages which suggest that any human being need only look within himself in order to discern these form-imposing faculties at work. In his Metaphysical Deduction of the Categories, for example, Kant refers to "synthesis in general" as "a blind but indispensable function of the soul, without which we should have no knowledge whatsoever, but of which we are scarcely ever conscious" (A78). Now just the idea that we *could* ever be conscious of this synthesizing activity, or that sometimes we *are* slightly aware of it, implies that it is something which is literally "in us" as human beings. It is, of course, imprudent to put great weight on any one passage in Kant, but to show Kant's psychological idiom in the first *Critique* we certainly need not do this, given the frequency of references to "we" and "us" and "human." George Schrader complains that many readers of Kant adopt a psychological interpretation of the a priori and that "many of the textbooks and a few of the commentaries" say that Kant regarded the faculty of sensibility on the model of colored glasses which are within the individual subject and through which the object of experience appears as spatial and temporal.[25] What Kant explicitly says throughout the *Critique*, however, makes it difficult to see how the reader could adopt any other interpretation.

Apart from the heavy use of human-psychological terminology, can we find anything which bears on this question in Kant's writing? One passage which seems strongly to support the individual-person interpretation of the Kantian subject is in the third Paralogism of the first edition, where Kant is speaking of the identity of the person (or soul) through time. He tells us that the identity which I attribute to myself as *subject* of *my* experience will be different from the kind of persistence through time which another person attributes to me as *object* of *his* experience. Remarking on this Kant says,

> For just as the time in which the observer sets me is not the time of my own but of his sensibility, so the identity which is necessarily bound up with my consciousness is not therefore bound up with his, that is, with the consciousness which contains the outer intuition of my subject. (A363)

This is the only passage in the first *Critique* in which Kant refers to different subjects as having numerically distinct faculties of sensibility.

---

[25]Schrader, "The Transcendental Ideality," 315.

Here he *seems* to be saying that just as I and an observer have our separate sensibilities, each has his own separate time.

In the second edition Paralogisms there is another passage which may be to the same effect. Kant says that the permanence of the soul cannot be known by anything which we are aware of in inner sense and then remarks, "Its permanence during life is, of course, evident per se, since the thinking being (as man) is itself likewise an object of the outer senses" (B415). This is the only acknowledgment anywhere in the first *Critique* that persons have bodies. In *The Bounds of Sense* P. F. Strawson attempts to build upon this rather slender base a proof of the necessary embodiment of persons, a proof which would certainly run counter to Kant's own view of what he had established.[26] But what exactly *is* Kant saying here? He tells us repeatedly that there is no inner intuition of the thinking subject—in this he agrees with Hume—and that therefore there is nothing to which the category of substance, or any other category, could be applied. For this reason we cannot even say that I appear to myself in inner sense as substantial, etc. But Kant seems to be saying here that the thinking subject *is* an object of *outer* sense to itself and to other subjects. To outer sense the subject appears as, presumably, a physical person. This material entity, this substance, has the same sort of phenomenal permanence which any material object has, and Kant *seems* to derive from this the view that the thinking subject must last at least as long its (living?) body does.

This may be simply an incautious statement on Kant's part which does not represent his considered view. More in line with the rest of Kant's philosophy is his statement slightly later in the *Critique* that "the subject, in which the representation of time has its original ground, cannot thereby determine its own existence in time" (B422), which implies that it is literally meaningless to ask how long the subject in itself (which is the source of time) lasts. What is relevant to our question, however, is the fact that Kant says here that the thinking subject—*each* thinking subject—appears to outer sense as a physical person. This admission by Kant indicates that on those few occasions when he is forced to consider the relation between "the subject" and human persons, Kant believes in a one-to-one relation between them.

---

[26]Strawson, *Bounds of Sense*, 162-69.

Can we find anything in the first *Critique* which seems to tell us that the form-imposing subject is *not* the individual knower? This task is rather more difficult. The most promising passages in this connection are those which speak of a single, "universal" consciousness and of the unity of the phenomenal world as a correlate of this. Kant tells us in the first edition Transcendental Deduction that

> there is one single experience in which all perceptions are represented as in thoroughgoing and orderly connection, just as there is only one space and one time in which all modes of appearance and all relations of being or not being occur. When we speak of different experiences, we can refer only to the various perceptions, all of which, as such belong to one and the same general experience. (A110)

Paton puzzles over this, as well he should, given his interpretation of Kant. He assures us that

> We must not take [Kant] to assert the reality of an all embracing divine experience, or to suggest that human experiences are part of such a divine experience.... We may affirm with confidence that doctrines of this type play no part in the Critical Philosophy.[27]

Yet Paton admits that "it is less easy to determine the precise character of the positive doctrine which Kant's own words are intended to convey," and he remarks that "curiously enough, Kant does not even ask how the experiences of different individual men are related to the one all-embracing experience."

Although the passage quoted above from the first edition of the *Critique* does not appear in the second edition, there are many passages in both editions which speak of the necessary unity of the phenomenal world and of there being one space and one time, and hence one order of physical objects in causal relation to one another. Kant holds that this unity of space and time is brought about by the productive imagination and is a correlate of the unity of consciousness. Now it seems disingenuous to insist as strongly as Kant does that there is one space-time world if all he means by this is that I perceive "the object" as being spatiotemporal, and so do you, and so does each other perceiving subject, that each of us has his own space and time, and that we all (to use Berkeley's phrase) agree in our perceptions. Indeed, to say the latter, that my

---

[27]Paton, *Kant's Metaphysics*, 2:427.

experiences cohere with yours, would mean even less for Kant under this interpretation than it does for Berkeley—for at least Berkeley has a single time in which all created spirits exist. But if Kant believes that each knower has his own time, it is hard to see what content could be given to the notion that my experiences correspond to, or cohere with, anyone else's. Yet one *could* interpret Kant this way. There is nothing in any of these statements about the unity of the phenomenal world which absolutely prevents the reader from saying that the Kantian unity of experience is just the unity of each subject's individual consciousness and that Kant's insistence upon a single world of appearance just means that "the object" appears to each of us as a single space-time order.

Since Kant never explicitly asks how many form-imposing subjects of experience there are, it is hopeless to attempt to find some particular passage which will force an answer to this question. The best strategy is to consider various general Kantian doctrines to see what they imply, or seem to imply, regarding the subject of experience. We have already seen that Kant's view of moral freedom, a priori knowledge, and the Antinomies push him toward equating the subject with the individual person. What Kant says about the difficulty of saying anything about subject or object in itself, plus his insistence on the unity of the phenomenal world, seem to push him just as strongly away from this view. To what else might we look?

The Causal Theory of Perception

The two different interpretations of the Kantian subject would seem to have quite contrasting implications regarding the causal theory of perception and the distinction between primary and secondary qualities which John Locke and others have drawn from this theory. If Kant believes that the subject is the individual person who is "affected" by the non-spatio-temporal object of his experience and who, because of his own cognitive faculties, apprehends this object as being in space and time, then we should expect that Kant, like Berkeley, would reject the causal theory of perception. If phenomenal objects *result from* the "given" manifold being acted upon by the mind, then they can hardly be the *cause of* this manifold through their action upon the sense organs. Some sort of contrast between primary and secondary qualities might still be salvaged under this view, but it would not be the distinction which Locke draws. As far as characterizing the apprehended object in its own intrinsic nature is concerned, all perceived or conceived qualities would be "secondary." We might say, however, that those qualities (or some of them) which Locke calls primary are those which this object necessarily appears to have for every subject of experience because of the cognitive faculties which are necessary for experience at all, whereas the secondary qualities are those which might vary from one subject to another.

Under the double affection interpretation, things would be simpler. If Kant takes this view of the subject of experience, then he could accept whatever story physiologists and psychologists wished to tell about the human mechanisms of perception. If, as Kemp Smith argues, the "given" manifold out of which the phenomenal world is created has no particular connection with the sensations in the minds of individual humans, then there is nothing to prevent Kant from accepting the scientific and common sense view that these sensations are caused by physical objects acting upon our sense organs. He could also accept whatever inferences a philosopher like Locke wished to derive from this view. Thus he could perfectly well say that certain perceived qualities really characterize physical objects in their own nature, whereas others characterize them only as they appear to human beings due to the human mechanisms of perception; but he would have to say also that this entire causal theory and its implications, while being (perhaps) perfectly true, had no relevance to what he was doing in the *Critique of Pure Reason*. Under the double affection interpretation, Kant would simply apply the label of "empirical" to this entire world described by the scientific realism of his day. He would say that this physical world, containing human percipients who perceive physical objects by interacting causally with them, is all only appearance. It is the appearance of "the object" to "the subject," neither of which has any special connection with human beings. Those features of the world which Kant discusses in the first *Critique* result from this subject (or these "underlying noumenal conditions") imposing space, time, causation, etc. upon the "given." The examination of how this comes about is the transcendental undertaking of the *Critique of Pure Reason*, and it is quite detached from any empirical enquiries about what goes on *within* this space-time world, including enquiries about how human beings perceive the things around them.

If these two interpretations of the Kantian subject have such contrasting implications regarding the causal theory of perception, it ought to be easy to see which view Kant himself takes just by seeing what he has to say about this theory and about the allied distinction between primary and secondary qualities. Unfortunately, what Kant has to say about this is extremely unclear, a fact which gives us further evidence that Kant is uncertain about how to relate his knowing subject to human persons. He first treats this topic at the end of the section on space in the Transcendental Aesthetic. He is concerned here to contrast his own doctrine of the subjectivity of space with what Locke says about the subjectivity of secondary qualities. In the first edition, he initially says something which sounds like the double affection view:

> The taste of a wine does not belong to the objective determinations of the wine, even if by the wine as object we mean the wine as appearance, but to the special constitution of sense in the subject that tastes it. Colors are not properties of the bodies to the intuition of which they are attached, but only modifications of the sense of sight, which is affected in a certain manner by light (A28).

So light does affect the "sense of sight" in a person, resulting in the physical object appearing as colored, even though these perceived colors are "not properties of the bodies" themselves. So far, this seems quite Lockean. In order to affect the sense of sight to produce these sensations of color, the body "in itself" must presumably really possess those features of size, shape, mass and so on, which Locke recognizes as primary qualities.

But with the very next sentence Kant appears to draw the primary-secondary quality distinction in accordance with the individual person interpretation of the subject of experience. He tells us that,

> Taste and colors [unlike space] are not necessary conditions under which alone objects can be for us objects of the senses. They are connected with the appearances only as effects accidentally added by the particular constitution of the sense organs. Accordingly, they are not a priori representations but are grounded in sensation. (A29)

In other words, neither color nor space characterizes what the subject—the individual person—is aware of in its own intrinsic nature. Both characterize the object only as it appears. But space is part of the "form" of appearance which *must be* imposed by the subject and hence is a priori knowable. It is a necessary condition of experience for any (human) subject that what the subject is aware of must appear as having spatial properties. Color, on the other hand, is part of sensation; hence it is due partly to the "matter" which is "given" to the subject and partly to those accidental features in the constitution of the subject which might well vary from one subject to another. Thus all perceivable and thinkable qualities characterize something only as it appears. Space and time, however, are ways in which the object *must* appear, whereas color is a way in which it just "accidentally" happens to appear.

Yet if we take the Kantian subject as individual person and then draw this sort of necessary-contingent distinction between the object's appearing as spatial and its appearing as colored, questions arise about the sense in which, for Kant, it *is* necessary for the object to appear as spatial. Kant does, after all, admit that other thinking beings may not have our forms of intuition and therefore may not perceive whatever they perceive as being in space. So in what sense are these forms necessary for us? If each of us has these modes of intuition, it is perhaps necessary that objects appear to us spatially, but likewise if a person has a certain physiology, then necessarily things will appear to him as colored. In both cases all that is necessary is that *if* a subject of experience has a certain constitution then things will appear to that subject in a certain way. Kant does not attempt to show in the first *Critique* that there is any necessity that we should have these particular forms of sensibility in the first place. Therefore, if the mind which imposes space is something which each individual possesses one of, then if all of our separate minds are similar in this respect, our agreement with regard to spatial perception will be as much a brute fact as the fact (if it is a fact) that we all perceive colors in the same way.

In his revised formulation in the second edition, Kant seems initially to stay with the interpretation of the subject as individual person and with the distinction between space and secondary qualities which follows from this. He says that we can have no a priori knowledge of color, sound, and heat, although our perceptions of the latter "agree with the representation of space, in this respect, that they belong merely to the subjective constitution of our manner of sensibility" (B44). Yet at the same time, Kant wishes to draw quite a sharp distinction between the subjectivity of space and that of color because he denies that "the ideality of space as here asserted can be illustrated by examples so altogether insufficient as colors, taste, etc." (B45). He says that the latter "cannot rightly be regarded as properties of things, but only as changes in the subject, changes which may, indeed, be different for different men" (B45). The implication of this would seem to be that space, by contrast, *is* a property of things, and that by means of these spatial characteristics physical objects act causally upon the sense organs of "different men" to produce sensations of color. Kant does not go so far as to say this, however. He tells us rather that the "empirical understanding" may treat an appearance, such as a rose, as if it were a thing in itself which could appear differently to different observers. He then reminds us "that nothing intuited in space is a thing in itself, that space is not a form of inhering in things in themselves as their intrinsic property," and so on.

I must confess that I cannot see a coherent view in all of this. Kant clearly wants to say that the object of experience necessarily appears as spatial and does not necessarily appear as colored. Yet it seems equally clear that he wants to say more than this. He wants to give the phenomenal object, at least in its Lockean primary qualities, a more solid, "real" status than it would have if it were only the manner in which the non-spatio-temporal object must appear to individual knowers. His only way of doing this would be to say that the form-imposing subject is *not* the individual knower; then he would be free to tell whatever Lockean story he wished about the human perception of physical objects.

In the Paralogisms section of the first edition of the *Critique*, there are strong indications that Kant intends the subject of experience to be the individual person, and therefore intends to reject at least the Lockean version of the causal theory of perception. He says, for example, that his doctrine secures "our thinking self against the danger of materialism" because with his discoveries about this thinking self,

> so completely are we freed from the fear that on the removal of matter all thought, and even the very existence of thinking beings, would be destroyed, that on the contrary it is clearly shown that if I remove the thinking subject the whole corporeal world must vanish: it is nothing save an appearance in the sensibility of our subject and a mode of its representations (A383).

So physical objects do not *cause* states of consciousness in the subject of experience. Rather, the dependence relation is just the reverse: the subject's consciousness is responsible for physical objects. Now this passage occurs in the context of a discussion of the immortality of the soul. Kant is looking ahead to his ethical writings and is attempting to insure that immortality as an article of rational faith will not be contradicted by anything in the sphere of theoretical reason. And surely the only sort of immortality which Kant is concerned with is personal immortality; he is not concerned here with any sort of cosmic Mind, still less with the "underlying noumenal conditions" of Kemp Smith. He wants to show that the individual you and I might be immortal, and so these must be the "thinking subjects" which are holding the phenomenal world in existence.

Shortly after this passage Kant discusses the rationalist's question of how movements in matter could be the cause of states of consciousness in the soul. He tells us that those representations which we call outer

> have, indeed, this deceptive property that, representing objects in space, they detach themselves as it were from the soul and appear to hover outside it. Yet this very space in which they are intuited is nothing but a representation, and no counterpart of the same quality is to be found outside the soul. (A385)

The fact that Kant uses the term "soul" (*Seele*) indicates that has in mind the individual person. He goes on to say that the problem about the causal relation between matter and mind rests upon the mistake of hypostatizing outer appearances and regarding physical objects as "things existing by themselves outside us, with the same quality as that with which they exist in us." If such were the case, Kant says, there would indeed be a problem, for

> in outer sense we find no outer effect save changes of place.... Within us, on the other hand, the effects are thoughts, among which is not to be found any relation of place, motion, shape or other spatial determination, and we altogether lose the thread of the causes in the effects to which they are supposed to have given rise in inner sense. (A386-87)

The solution of this is to understand that

> neither bodies nor motions are anything outside us; both alike are mere representations in us; and it is not, therefore, the motion of matter that produces representations in us; the motion itself is representation only, as also is the matter which makes itself known in this way. (A387)

The failure of philosophers to see this is the result of "judgments in which a misapprehension has taken deep root through long custom," the misapprehension, namely, that physical objects exist independently of our consciousness.

Two things about this passage call for comment. First, it is hard to see how Kant could be more clear or explicit in his rejection of the causal theory of perception. Second, it is interesting that Kant does not attempt to say about his philosophy what Berkeley says about his. Berkeley makes the dubious, although no doubt sincere, claim that his philosophy does not contradict anything which the "ordinary man" believes about the world. Berkeley believes that his own theory accepts a common sense view of the world and then tells an additional story about how this real world of trees, houses, and other "things" (ideas) depends upon the continuous omniscience of God. If Kant were to take the double affection view of his form-imposing subject, he might say something analogous about his own theories, substituting the scientific realist such as Locke or Newton for Berkeley's ordinary man. We would expect him to say, perhaps, that the Lockean view of the world, or something like it, is perfectly true and that the doctrines of the first *Critique* are not intended in any way to contradict it. Kant's philosophy under this interpretation would be an additional, "transcendental" story *about* this real space-time world, explaining the necessity of certain features of it and the source of this necessity in the mental activity of "the subject." In this first edition Paralogisms section, however, Kant certainly says nothing of the sort. He tells us that not only the ordinary man's view of the world but also the scientist's belief in an independent world of material objects is *wrong*. It is wrong because of the "deceptive property" of certain of our states of mind, a property which has given rise to this "misapprehension" (which has taken "deep root") that there exists a space-time world independent of our individual minds.

Perhaps we should not put too much weight on these passages, for among adherents of the patchwork theory of the composition of the first *Critique*, the first edition Paralogisms are a favorite candidate for the appellation of "pre-Critical." This section is the most Berkeleyan sounding part of the *Critique of Pure of Reason*, and it was completely rewritten for the second edition. We must ask, though, if it is actually contradicted by anything in the second edition of the *Critique*. The answer is that it *seems* to go against the conclusion of the Refutation of Idealism, which is found only in the second edition. Here, and in the second of the Analogies of Experience (which is largely the same in both editions), Kant appears to want to give the phenomenal world a more solidly real status than that of being only representations in the minds of individual subjects. Now if in the Kantian philosophy the space-time world is something which exists independently of human beings, then of course it cannot be these human persons who are the source of space, time, and so on; it must be some other "subject," and we are back into the double affection view. It is dubious, however, to attribute any such direction to Kant's thought from the first to the second edition of the *Critique*. For we do have Kant's assertion in the preface to the second edition that there had been no alteration in his philosophical views (Bxxxvii-xlii). Also, there is the fact that even though the second edition as a whole sounds somewhat less subjectivist (in Kemp Smith's sense of this term) than the first edition, the difference here is only one of degree; there are plenty of passages in both editions which suggest that the Kantian subject is the individual you and I, and that space and time are nothing outside of "us."

Finally, even though the Refutation of Idealism seems to contradict the individual-person interpretation of the Kantian subject, we really need to understand the argument here if we are to be sure of what Kant intends as its conclusion, and such understanding is not easy. The Refutation of Idealism is dealt with in the second section of this essay, in which I examine Kant's conception of the relation of consciousness to its object. Let me just say here that it is only with substantial "squeezing" that we may see the Refutation of Idealism as actually contradicting the first edition Paralogisms. It is more likely that Kant felt some dissatisfaction with the subjectivist, even Berkeleyan, tone of parts of the first edition and wanted to de-emphasize this tone in the second edition, but that he did not develop any positive alternative (and certainly not the double affection theory) to substitute for his original view that the form-imposing subject of experience is the individual person. One indication of this can be found in the *Prolegomena*, which was written after the first edition of the first *Critique*. In his only discussion of secondary qualities in this work, Kant defends his idealism as being simply an extension of what Locke says about colors and sounds. It is a matter of scientific common sense, Kant says, that certain properties of objects, such as colors, characterize the objects only as they appear because of the perceptual apparatus of the subject: "Now, if I go farther and, for weighty reasons, rank as mere appearances the remaining qualities of bodies also, which are called primary . . . no one can in the least adduce the reason if its being is inadmissable" (289-90 in the Academy edition). Here the subject whose cognitive apparatus makes things appear spatial and temporal is obviously regarded by Kant as the same one to whom things appear as colored, namely the individual person.

The "I Think." Phenomena and Noumena

Another section of the *Critique of Pure Reason* which would seem to bear upon the identity of Kant's form-imposing subject is the discussion in the Transcendental Deduction of the "I think" and its relation to the unity of consciousness. At A107 Kant distinguishes between transcendental apperception and empirical apperception. The latter is simply my awareness of the contents of my own mind, perceived through the form of inner sense which is time. Kant tells us that "No fixed and abiding self can present itself in this flux of inner appearances." Transcendental apperception, by contrast, is a "pure unchangeable consciousness" which Kant later describes as a consciousness of "the complete identity of the self in respect of all representations which can ever belong to our knowledge" (A116). This consciousness contains "the bare representation "I" in relation to all other representations"; transcendental consciousness is the origin of my sense of myself as one subject of experience and is what allows for a single awareness of a single, unified world.

In the B edition Deduction, however, Kant emphasizes that "through the "I" as simple representation, nothing manifold is given; only in intuition, which is distinct from the "I," can a manifold be given; and only through *combination* in one consciousness can it be thought" (B135). This "I" of transcendental consciousness is therefore not any sort of object or "thing" at all. For this reason it makes no sense to ask what kind of thing it is, whether it is the human person or a cosmic Mind or anything else. In the Paralogisms Kant makes the point repeatedly that because the representation "I" or "I think" is neither an intuition nor a concept—only a "bare consciousness which accompanies all concepts" (A346)—it cannot be used to give us any insight into the intrinsic nature of ourselves. For this reason Kant's remarks on transcendental (and empirical) self-consciousness do not provide any answer to the question, which remains a legitimate one, of how the form-imposing "mind" of Kant's Copernican Revolution is supposed to relate to human beings.[28]

The only other part of the first *Critique* which might be relevant to our question is the section on Phenomena and Noumena, which will be discussed in some detail in the second part of this essay. Here it is sufficient to point out that this is the only place in the *Critique of Pure Reason* in which Kant describes a subject of experience which is definitely not the individual human being. This is the hypothetical being with intellectual intuition whose understanding literally creates its own

---

[28]For an excellent discussion of Kant's theory of self-consciousness and his attacks on rational psychology, see Wilfred Sellars's "This I or He or It (the Thing) Which Thinks," *Proceedings of the American Philosophical Association* 44 (1970–1971): 5-31. See also Karl Ameriks's *Kant's Theory of Mind* (Oxford: Clarendon Press, 1982).

object in thinking it. Such a being would not have to wait passively for sensory "matter" to be "given" and, therefore, would have no need for a faculty of sensibility. Contrasted with this being is the sort of knower who does not have this faculty of creative understanding but who must receive sensory data through the forms of sensibility (which are space and time) and who is therefore presented with a sensory manifold. The understanding of such a subject, not being intuitive, must be discursive, which is to say that it must function by synthesizing the manifold of given data into a single consciousness.

The contrast which Kant draws here, between a being with an intuitive understanding and one with a discursive understanding, looks very much like an epistemological version of the contrast between God and human beings. (At B72 of the *Critique* Kant says that as far as we can tell only "the primordial being" possesses an intuition which creates its own object.) The latter sort of subject is obviously limited, or finite, since it does not have the creative cognitive faculties of the former. If one were committed to the double affection view, one *could* recognize three different subjects in Kant: the possible being with intellectual intuition, another being with a passive, discursive understanding (the subject whose activity generates the space-time world), plus individual persons. Such a multiplication of subjects is quite implausible as an interpretation of Kant, however, and there is certainly no clue in the section on Phenomena and Noumena that this was Kant's intention. Rather, Kant must have intended this limited knower, who is passive in respect to his reception of sensory data, to be "we" finite human beings.

Conclusion
Kant's View of the Knowing Subject
The "Empirical Reality" of Space and Time

In describing the options which seem to be open to Kant regarding the relation of the form-imposing "subject" to individual human beings, I have presented two extreme possibilities for interpreting Kant: either a strict identity between this subject and individual persons or a cosmic status for the subject, in which the cognitively active creative mind will have no more relation to human beings and their empirically studied activities than it will to anything else in the universe. It has been suggested to me that these need not be the only options available to Kant, that Kant might assert a "partial identity" between his creative subject and human beings, or that he might simply leave the question of this relationship completely open. Kant could perhaps say that there must be some relationship which, we being the limited creatures which we are, is forever beyond human comprehension.

There may indeed be a third way open to Kant, although Kant does not present us with any such solution in his published writings. My criticism of Kant is that he does not seem to adopt any view at all of the relation of the form-imposing subject of experience to human beings, and he needs to take *some* position on this question if he is to make clear his distinctively Kantian "transcendental" form of idealism and to distinguish it from the idealism of Berkeley. It is remarkable that in the entire text of the *Critique of Pure Reason* and the *Prolegomena*, even in all of his statements of his Copernican Revolution, Kant never asks himself what the relationship is between a human being and the "mind" which is the source of space, time, causal connection, and all the rest. It is wrong say that Kant held anything like the later Idealist view of a cosmic Mind or World-Soul as the source of the phenomenal world. There were certainly factors pushing him in this direction, but to say that he actually held such a view requires that we do violence to the text. It is more accurate to say that he originally intended his subject of experience to be the individual person, that he came to see the problems which were involved in this view, and that he never arrived at any final, definitive position on this question.

Strawson complains in his commentary of Kant's "neglect of the empirical concept of a subject of experience" and remarks that Kant "barely alludes" to the fact that persons have bodies.[29] Kant may, however, have realized that if he had dealt at all with physical, embodied persons, he would have been led to questions for which he had no answer. In any case, Kant's uncertainty over what to say about the subject of experience is mirrored in an uncertainty over the reality of the space-time world. The different interpretations of the Kantian subject will result in different forms of idealism, with very different implications about what it can mean to say that the physical world is real; furthermore, only the double affection view would enable us to say that the world is real in any sense which corresponds at all to our ordinary beliefs. Of course, there are difficulties in such an interpretation apart from those which we have

---

[29]Strawson, *Bounds of Sense*, 169 and 164.

already seen. This interpretation of Kant seems to involve the notion that we are all in some sense "within the mind" of some cosmic Subject and that we and objects around us are part of this universal consciousness. I am not at all sure that I could make such an idea even intelligible, let alone plausible; and it is especially dubious for such a doctrine to be attributed to Kant because it looks very much like the sort of transcendent metaphysics which the first *Critique* was intended to repudiate. (See below, chap. 6, A.) But at least under this interpretation we can say that our world is real in the sense that we all live together in it and that we are products of it, rather than the reverse. Under the double affection view of Kant's knowing subject, the world which I live in and am conscious of exists independently of me as a particular human being and independently of human beings in general; and this is surely a minimum condition of this world being real in any ordinary sense.

Suppose we say that the Kantian subject is the individual knower, of whom I am one and you are another. If each of us imposes his own space and time on his own "given" data, then the space-time world of my experience will be numerically distinct from the space-time world of yours. Furthermore, each of our separate phenomenal worlds will be nothing apart from that particular subject's consciousness. When the subject loses consciousness, his or her phenomenal world qua space-time order will vanish. It may be true that the object which the subject was aware of will remain, but that space-time world which was the appearance of the of the object *to* that particular subject will disappear when the subject does. The only thing which "empirically real" could then mean when applied to the space-time world is that each of our individual centers or "streams" of consciousness is required to exist, or occur, in certain ways. And this, surely, is a long way from any ordinary conception of physical reality.

The question of the nature of Kant's idealism, and the "reality" of his space-time world, will be dealt with further in the next section of this essay, where I discuss Kant's view of the relation of consciousness to its object and deal with what Kant says about our conception of reality per se and how this concept functions in our experience. From what has been said so far, however, it should be evident that because of his uncertainty over the status of the subject of experience, if for no other reason, there is a deep unclarity in Kant's idealism which prevents Kant from having a single doctrine about how real the physical world is. In place of any one coherent doctrine, all we have are Kant's assurances that although this world is ideal in a transcendental sense, it is after all "empirically" real.

Chapter 3

The Relation of Consciousness to Its Object

The Background of Kant's Question

The second question which bears upon our inquiry about the kind of idealism which Kant espouses is that of what it means, in Kant's view, to say that the subject's consciousness is of an object. What, exactly, is this outward-referring "of" status which consciousness is supposed to have? This issue can be treated largely independently of our question about the status of the subject itself because an answer to the one question does not logically necessitate any particular answer to the other. Yet there may be some de facto links between the possible answers to these questions in terms of what Kant intended for his own philosophy. These links will be explored in this second section.

To see how Kant interprets the thesis that consciousness has an object, I find it useful to regard Kant's philosophy, or part of it, as a response to a central perplexity in Descartes's *Meditations*. Kant was familiar with the writings of Descartes and refers to Descartes several times in his own work. It is reasonable to suppose that parts of Kant's philosophy are intended as a response to Descartes as much as to Hume.[1]

---

[1] Reasonable, but not certain. See Margaret Wilson's "Kant and the Refutations of Subjectivism," in L. W. Beck, *Kant's Theory of Knowledge* (Dordrecht: Reidel, 1974) 208-17. Wilson argues here that Cartesian scepticism about the external world was not a major concern of Kant in the first *Critique*. Consider also that Kant says in the long note in the preface to the *second* edition of this *Critique* that "it still remains a scandal to philosophy . . . that the existence of things outside us . . . must be accepted merely on *faith*" (Bxl). This note suggests Kant was not greatly concerned with Cartesian skepticism during his initial writing of

In any case, Descartes's question, stated in non-Cartesian terminology, is this: Given that I exist as the subject of my experience, and given that I am possessed of states of consciousness (or "representations" or "ideas") as facts about myself, how do I know that this is not all there is? I normally assume that in addition to myself and my consciousness there exists an object *of* my consciousness, a real world with which my consciousness puts me in contact. Some of my states of consciousness, I suppose, have this kind of outward (from myself) reference, such that they constitute an awareness *of* some object. But how, we may ask, can I know that this is so? How can I be sure that my states of consciousness are not states of myself and nothing more and that I with my consciousness am not the totality of what there is?

In posing this problem Descartes feels that the question itself is quite clear. He believes that we know perfectly well what expressions such as "object of consciousness" and "real world" mean and that we know what it means to say that my consciousness, or some of it, is "of" such an objective order. The only question for Descartes is whether or not this situation obtains, whether I am in fact conscious of an object, and how I can be sure that I am. Kant, however, does not assume throughout the *Critique of Pure Reason* that this question is perfectly clear. There are places, especially in the Transcendental Deduction and in the second of the Analogies of Experience, where Kant addresses himself to the question of what it *means* to say that one's consciousness is "of an object."

Now in contrast to his silence about the identity of the knowing subject, Kant has a great deal to say in answer to this second question. One of the things which make the *Critique of Pure Reason* such a difficult work, however, is that Kant has two quite different stories to tell in answer to this question of what it means for consciousness to have an object. He presents what I will call, for lack of any better expressions, a correspondence and a coherence theory of the outward reference of consciousness. These two views are quite different and incompatible, but they are both maintained in the first *Critique*. I will argue later that Kant's adherence to these incompatible theories, as well as his uncertainty about the subject of experience, result from the conflicting demands of his doctrines of perception and thought. (See below, chap. 5.) For the

---

the *Critique of Pure Reason*, even though his philosophy in this first edition may, as Strawson and others believe, be very relevant to the Cartesian question.

present, we must consider these two theories of consciousness themselves and the different forms of idealism and different views of physical reality which they imply.

Kant's Correspondence Theory of Consciousness

It is useful to state Kant's correspondence view of consciousness baldly here and then to give the textual evidence for it.[2] According to this theory consciousness involves a relationship between two ontologically distinct things, the subject of experience plus what we may call simply the object. This relationship which we call, from the side of the subject, the subject's *consciousness of* the object is the very same relationship which may, from the side of the object, be called the object's *appearance to* the subject. The Kantian subject is of course not a blank tablet, but has an elaborate cognitive apparatus through which it apprehends the object, and we may therefore distinguish the object of awareness as it is in its own intrinsic nature from this same object as it appears to the subject. At this point the distinction is only a logical one which would not prevent the object from appearing to the subject exactly as it is in itself. What makes the distinction more significant is Kant's view of the form-imposing nature of "our" mental faculties. The forms of sensibility are space and time, as a result of which what is "given" to the subject, prior to the subject's conceptual activities upon it, is a multiplicity of sensory data which Kant refers to as a manifold. This manifold must then be synthesized by the understanding into a single conscious experience. The result of this mental activity is that the object appears to the subject as a world of material things in space and time.

Kant is quite insistent that space, time, causation, and all the rest do not characterize the object as it is in itself but rather only as it appears, but many commentators have wondered how Kant could be so sure about

---

[2]This view is described well by Strawson in the section of *The Bounds of Sense* entitled "The Metaphysics of Transcendental Idealism" (235-73). Strawson fails to do justice, however, to the other, "necessary connection," view of consciousness that is equally present in the text. The reason for this, I think, is that this other Kantian interpretation of "of an object" is part of Kant's doctrine of synthesis and hence is tied up with what Strawson calls Kant's "imaginary subject" of transcendental psychology, which Strawson feels can be deleted without harm to anything of value in Kant's philosophy.

this and have argued that a better Kantian position would be one of agnosticism on this point. The long controvery over the non-spatiality (and non-temporality, etc.) of the thing in itself has been abetted by Kant's failure to address this question in any very explicit and systematic manner anywhere in his writings. Kant does say in the *Prolegomena* that we cannot say that the object of awareness in its own nature, independent of the subject's awareness of it, exists in time and space because "it is palpably contradictory to say that a mere mode of representation exists without our representation" (341-42 in the Academy edition). This sounds somewhat like Berkeley's argument that only an idea can resemble another idea, but the argument is not developed enough for us to be sure of what Kant has in mind here.

Probably the best strategy for Kant to use would be based on the space-time Antinomies. If we assume that the law of non-contradiction applies to the thing in itself (such that this object in its own nature could not possess contradictory attributes) and if Kant's arguments are correct that if the world were spatial and temporal in its own nature, it would necessarily both have and not have spatial limits plus a temporal beginning and also be both infinitely divisible and composed of atoms, these arguments would suffice to show that a thing in its own nature cannot be in space and time. And if our concepts of substance, cause, and the rest of Kant's categories are meaningful only when applied to a space-time "manifold"—another debated question in Kant scholarship—then these features likewise could not characterize anything in itself. Kant realized the possibility of using the arguments of the Antinomies in this way, for he says that it is a "critical and doctrinal" advantage of this self-contradictory character of space and time considered as things in themselves that "it affords indirect proof of the transcendental ideality of appearances" (A506).

This is sufficient, I believe, to refute the double aspect interpretation of Kant's thing in itself, which has had a number of advocates in recent years. According to this interpretation Kant does not argue that there actually *is* anything which in any sense lies behind or beyond the space-time world. He says only that *if* there were, we could have no knowledge of it. This seems to be the view taken by Graham Bird, who argues in his commentary that Kant "recognized that his key term "appearance" had a special sense different from its conventional empirical meaning, since it stipulated rather than described the objects given to us in perception."³ The term "appearance," then, is just a sort of proper ("stipulative," non-descriptive) name for whatever we may meet with in experience. Kant's use of this term, according to Bird, is intended only to "limit the range of our possible experience to objects which can be presented to the senses," rather than to assert positively that there *is* anything other than the physical universe. This view of the thing in itself is also put forward in an article by Henry Allison entitled, "The Non-Spatiality of Things in Themselves for Kant."⁴ Here Allison argues that the statement "things in themselves are non-spatial," is merely definitional and that for Kant the thing in itself is just the object of our awareness considered "transcendentally," i.e., considered apart from those features (space, time, causality, etc.) which render it capable of being experienced by us. Strawson argues very well in *The Bounds of Sense* that although such a modest interpretation of Kant may at times be a possible reading of some portions of the text, it fails utterly to do justice to Kant's philosophy as a whole.⁵

So for whatever reasons, Kant does believe that what the subject is aware of in its own nature is not spatio-temporal, etc., but only appears to be, due to the nature of the knowing subject. This would pretty much suffice as an exposition of Kant's correspondence, or relational, view of consciousness were it not for the fact that there is another story which Kant tells within this general framework. This additional story complicates the situation considerably. Usually Kant speaks as though what the subject is aware of is simply "the object," although not as it is in itself but rather only as it appears. Kant also, however, speaks of the object "affecting" the subject to produce "representations," states of mind which are somehow within the subject himself. These representations are then identified as appearances and become objects in their own right, the immediate objects of perceptual awareness. (Kant speaks this way, among other places, in those passages where he is trying to make clear the

---

³Graham Bird, *Kant's Theory of Knowledge* (New York: Humanities Press, 1962) 49-50.

⁴Henry Allison, "The Non-Spatiality of Things in Themselves for Kant," *Journal of the History of Philosophy* 14 (1976): 313-21. This view is further developed and elaborated in Allison's "epistemological" interpretation of Kant's transcendental idealism. I examine this view below, in chap. 6, sec. B.

⁵Strawson, *Bounds of Sense*, 19-33, 51-54.

"transcendental" nature of his own version of idealism. See above, Ch. I.B.) Kant then says, or seems to say, that appearances and the thing in itself are ontologically distinct things and that the object of consciousness is appearance (or the space-time world) which stands in the relation of being *produced by* this other object (the thing in itself) of which we can know nothing.

Such a view would seem to be modeled upon Locke's notion that physical objects cause "ideas" in the mind of the subject and that these ideas are all that the subject directly apprehends. The difficulties of any such doctrine in the context of Kant's philosophy are obvious to beginning readers of Kant, given his assertion that our concept of cause applies only within experience. For this reason it is tempting to suppose that Kant never intended to say anything like this but was simply careless in some of the statements of his theory. This is the line taken by Paton, always the sympathetic interpreter of Kant. He tells us that Kant's "primary view" is that "things as they are in themselves are the very same things that appear to us. . . . Strictly speaking, there are not two things, but only one thing considered in two different ways: the thing as it is in itself and as it appears to us."[6] Paton admits that Kant also speaks, "less happily," of things in themselves affecting our sensibility and producing appearances or ideas, but Paton says only that this misleading "usage" is "natural and difficult to avoid," not that it shows any real confusion in Kant.

This question of whether in Kant's philosophy we are aware of "the object" itself (albeit only as it appears), or whether we are immediately conscious of *other* things (appearances) which are *produced by* "the object," is given a good treatment in an article by S.F. Barker, who distinguishes between the "language of appearing" and the "language of appearances."[7] In the first of these languages, awareness or consciousness is assumed to be of an independently existing object; once this point is understood, one can then draw whatever distinction one wishes between the object as it appears and this same object as it is in itself. In the language of appearance, however, appearance becomes an entity in own right, one which the subject "immediately" apprehends. In this way of

---

[6] Paton, *Kant's Metaphysics*, 1:61-62.
[7] S. F. Barker, "Appearing and Appearances in Kant," *Monist* 51 (1967): 426-41.

speaking, appearances are equated with states of mind (or ideas, or sense-data) of the subject. They are private to the individual subject—only *I* can perceive *this* appearance—and they can exist only while they are being perceived. Holding this view, one may then choose to tell an additional story to the effect that these appearance or ideas in the mind are caused by other things acting on the mind through the sense organs (or the "sensibility").

Barker rightly feels that these two "languages" are not just two philosophically neutral, interchangeable ways of saying the same thing. Rather, they represent altogether different views of consciousness and the object of consciousness. Barker also claims that in the *Critique of Pure Reason* Kant uses both of these languages without ever explicitly distinguishing between them. This would explain, among other things, Kant's unquestioning acceptance of the thing in itself. Throughout most of the first *Critique* Kant does not feel that he needs to argue for the existence of the thing in itself at all, and this is puzzling if the thing in itself is viewed as the cause of appearances in the mind of the subject. If one assumes the language of appearing, however, and assumes that consciousness is of an independent object, then the thing in itself will be just this very object in its own nature, and no particular argument for this thing *in itself* will be required.

A look at the first *Critique* and the *Prolegomena* shows that one can find, as Barker says, a wealth of statements illustrating each of these two views of appearance. In my own analysis of these works, I have found that the language of appearing in fact predominates. There is, however, enough of the language of appearance to leave no doubt that Kant held this view as well. We might call these two versions of the correspondence theory (1) the theory of the object as "that which appears," and (2) the theory of the object as "cause of appearance." There is no doubt that the first version makes much more sense than the second in terms of the rest of Kant's philosophy, and this raises the question of why Kant held the second view at all. To this question I can only speculate that perhaps Kant was so imbued with the philosophy and science of his day, which spoke of perceptions in the mind being caused by spatially external objects or by God or by a possible evil demon, that he could not altogether liberate himself from it even when engaged in his own quite different enterprise. Kant's doctrine of synthesis may also have pushed him toward this "language of appearance" view. For if synthesis is construed as any sort of literal activity or process of binding together a given multiplicity of items, then it would seem more intelligible to regard these items as mental contents produced from without, rather than as object(s)-as-they-appear.

Both of these views of the object, as that which appears and as cause of appearance, I regard as alternate versions of Kant's correspondence theory of consciousness. I should emphasize here that when I attribute a correspondence view of consciousness to Kant, the notion of correspondence which I am employing is a modest one. I intend to say only that in this strand of his thinking Kant regards the subject and the object as two distinct things and that he regards the subject's knowledge of the object as involving a relation between these two entities. To flesh out the notion of correspondence slightly—but only slightly—we could say that in the subject's knowledge of the object, the subject's consciousness is the way it is (in part) *because of* the way the object is. To say anything further than this about resemblance or one-to-one relations between states of the subject and properties of the object would be a mistake. Taking this pared down conception of correspondence, I would argue that such a view of consciousness most easily arises if one thinks about consciousness or experience "from the outside" as occurring in a subject other than oneself. If I am considering another subject of experience and I ask what the difference is between this subject merely "having" consciousness as an attribute of himself and same subject really being aware *of* some object or situation, it seems obvious that in the latter case there must be some independent thing existing apart from the subject to which the subject is somehow related. A weakness of this view of consciousness, however, is that it does not even begin to answer Descartes's central question in his first *Meditation*. For if one *assumes* that consciousness is a relationship between two separate things and that it therefore connects the subject to an independent object or realm of objects, all that remains is the question of whether or not this object appears to us exactly as it is in its own nature. Descartes does not ask this question until the sixth *Meditation*, where he gives an account which resembles somewhat the later Lockean theory of primary and secondary qualities. The question which concerns Descartes throughout the *Meditations* is whether consciousness is "of an object" in this correspondence or relational sense at all. When he is adhering to his correspondence view of consciousness in the first *Critique*, Kant simply assume what Descartes doubts and then devotes his energies to the other question of whether and to what extent we are aware of the object as it is in its own inherent nature.

A final point which we may make about Kant's correspondence theory of consciousness is that if we adopt this view and retain our normal use of "real" and its cognates, we will identify reality, in Kant's philosophical system, with the thing in itself. The space-time world, being contrasted with the thing in itself, will be in *some* sense unreal. We must be careful in our choice of terms here and not attribute to Kant's phenomenal world any such derogatory status as that of being a dream, illusion, or hallucination, even though some commentators have taken this interpretation.[8] But when Kant tells us that space and time do not characterize what we are aware of as it is in its own nature but rather only as it appears to us, this seems tantamount to saying that reality is non-spatio-temporal.

Much of the literature on Kant takes this line and does not hesitate to apply the terms "real" or "reality" to the thing in itself. Paton, for example, addresses himself to the question of the "relation of appearances to reality" in Kant's philosophy and suggests that Kant "probably regarded reality [in contrast to he space-time world] as made up of monads."[9] Kemp Smith tells us that for Kant both physical objects and states of consciousness in time are appearances and that "neither can be identified with the absolutely real."[10] He also attributes to Kant the criticism of Berkeleyan idealism that it "virtually denies the existence of the only true reality, that of things in themselves."[11] Robert Paul Wolff tells us in his commentary that for Kant, "the phrase 'thing in itself' is, I think, simply a synonym for 'independently real thing'."[12] And Strawson says that Kant's doctrine is "not merely that we can have no knowledge of a supersensible reality. The doctrine is that reality is super-

---

[8] Schopenhauer, e.g., praises Kant for expressing "in an entirely new and original way" the Indian doctrine that "this sensible world in which we are [is] a magic effect called into being, an unstable and inconsistent illusion without substance, comparable to the optical illusion and the dream." "Criticism of the Kantian Philosophy," an addendum to *The World as Will and Representation*, trans. E. F. J. Payne (New York: Dover Publications, 1969) 1:419.

[9] Paton, *Kant's Metaphysics*, 1:183.

[10] Kemp Smith, *Commentary*, 139.

[11] Ibid., 159.

[12] Wolff, *Kant's Theory of Mental Activity* (Cambridge MA: Harvard University Press, 1963), 313.

sensible and that we can have no knowledge of it."[13] Yet it is interesting that unlike these commentators, Kant himself is quite circumspect in his use of terms such as "real" and "objective reality." Although he continually characterizes the physical world as (only) appearance, it is less often that he takes what would seem to be the obvious next step and says that the thing in itself constitutes reality. And he never, either in the first *Critique* or the *Prolegomena*, says that the space-time world is *not* real. He does, of course, say that it is transcendentally ideal, but given Kant's view of what the reality of anything amounts to, "ideal" here should not be taken to mean "unreal." To see why this is so and to see how Kant handles the concept of objective reality generally, we must examine Kant's second theory of the outward reference of consciousness, his coherence theory.

Phenomena and Noumena

Before we enter into this theory, there is one further portion of the first *Critique* which is of interest in connection with Kant's correspondence view of consciousness. It is the section of the Analytic of Principles entitled, "The Ground of the Distinction of All Objects in General into Phenomena and Noumena." Those commentators who subscribe to the patchwork theory of the composition of the first *Critique* regard this as among the earlier parts of this work. In any case, it contains a particularly strong statement of the correspondence theory. Kant says in the A edition that it follows from the very "concept of an appearance in general" that

> something which is not itself appearance must correspond to it . . . the word appearance must be recognized as already indicating a relation to something, the immediate representation of which is, indeed, sensible, but which . . . must be something in itself, that is, an object independent of our sensibility. (A251-2)

To this something in itself, the thing in itself, Kant gives the name "noumenon." But in Kant's doctrine of the noumenon as put forward in the first edition of the *Critique* and as modified in the second, we see another doctrine emerging. This new doctrine is something over and above the simple view that consciousness is of an object and that this object must

---

[13]Strawson, *Bounds of Sense*, 38.

have some (real) nature of its own apart from our experience of it. It is the idea that to *be* at all is to be the object of some sort of intuition. Kant's conception of the noumenon, as expressed in the first edition of the *Critique*, unites these two doctrines. For after giving us the above account of the "object independent of our sensibility," Kant goes on to say,

> But in order that a noumenon may signify a true object, distinguishable from all phenomena, it is not enough that I *free* my thought from all conditions of sensible intuition; I must likewise have ground for *assuming* another kind of intuition, different from the sensible, in which such an object may be given. (A252)

Kant's uniting of two conceptions here—of the noumenon as the real, inherent nature of that which appears to us and also as the object of an intuition different from ours—is most clearly expressed in the following passage:

> For if the senses represent to us something merely *as it appears*, this something must also in itself be a thing, and an object of a non-sensible intuition, that is, of the understanding. In other words, a knowledge must be possible, in which there is no sensibility, and which alone has reality that is absolutely objective. Through it objects will be represented *as they are*, whereas in the empirical employment of our understanding things will be known only *as they appear*. (A249)

This line of thought is quite remarkable and does not, as far as I know, appear elsewhere in Kant's writings. Kant comes close to accepting the following argument: "Our" cognitive faculties are distorting in that our understanding is discursive rather than intuitive. This is to say that it does not generate its own sensory data, but must be given data from without. The sensibility is the capacity of the mind to receive such data through being affected by the object of awareness. The forms of sensibility are space and time, and because space and time consist of distinguishable parts, these data are presented as a manifold which requires a synthesis by the understanding acting through the intermediate faculty of imagination. The categories are the rules by which this synthesis is performed, resulting in a single consciousness of one space-time realm. Because of the Antinomies, however, we can be sure that space and time do not characterize the object of our awareness as it is in itself. Therefore, there must be an intrinsic nature of this object which is unknown to us.

Kant seems to say at this point that to *be* at all, to exist as a real thing, it is necessary to be the object of some intuition. Therefore, this object as it is in itself, this nature which is unknown to us, must be known through some other kind of intuition, one which, unlike ours, is non-distorting. This other kind of intuition, and hence the being which has this intuition, is necessary to hold the thing in itself, or noumenon, in existence. The conclusion of this argument would seem to be that there must exist some sort of cosmic Mind, analogous to Berkeley's God in its sustaining mental activity but holding up our phenomenal world only indirectly through its sustaining intuition of that object in itself of which our space-time world is the appearance.

Kant does not, of course, finally embrace such a view. In the first edition, immediately after describing this other, intellectual kind of intuition, he goes on to say that not only do *we* not have such an intuition, but we have no way of knowing whether any other being has it. Indeed, we cannot know that such a way of intuiting is even possible, and so "it is still an open question whether this notion of a noumenon [i.e., the object of a non-sensible intuition] be not a mere form of a concept" (A253). In the second edition Kant makes a distinction which better enables him to express these views. He defines noumenon in the negative sense as, "a thing in so far as it is not an object of our sensible intuition." This is simply the object in its own nature, the thing in itself, to which Kant's correspondence theory of consciousness has committed him. Noumenon in a positive sense is "an object of a non-sensible [intellectual] intuition" (B307). Belief in such an object entails a belief in this mode of intuition, and since our own cognitive faculties are such that we "cannot comprehend even the possibility" of such an intuition, Kant tells us that what we call noumenon "must be understood as being such only in a *negative* sense" (B309).

It is not hard to see the reason for Kant's ambivalence here. The notion that to be at all is to be the object of some intuition is evidently very persuasive to Kant. He sees, however, that to carry out the implications of this principle and to posit some sort of Mind unlike ours holding the world as it is in itself in being by thinking it via His intellectual intuition would be the sort of excursion into transcendent metaphysics which is forbidden to us by what Kant says about *our* understanding and its ability to think about anything. Kant therefore draws back and says that we cannot prove that this other kind of intuition is even possible. So he is committed only to the notion of noumenon in the negative sense, the object of our awareness as it is in itself. Regarding the noumenon in a positive sense, this thing in itself as object of some other, intellectual intuition, Kant remains tentative and noncommittal because of his inability, given the constraints of his own system, to take any stronger stand.

What conclusions may we draw from this entire section on Phenomena and Noumena? I have pointed out earlier (see above, 41-42) that this part of the *Critique* seems to lend support to the interpretation of the Kantian subject as the individual person because of its contrast between the hypothetical being with an intuitive understanding and the being with the other, limited kind of understanding which is discursive.[14] We may also mention that the view of consciousness which we find here is predominantly Kant's correspondence or relational view. From the standpoint of the finite, discursive intellect, this correspondence theory is clear from Kant's adherence to noumena in the negative sense. But even from the standpoint of the intuitive understanding, it seems that some sort of correspondence view of "of an object" must be taken. For the coherence or necessary-connection view of the relation of consciousness to its object is based on Kant's doctrine of synthesis. This doctrine, in turn, would seem to require the notion of a sensory manifold, the elements of which need to be brought together by the understanding working through the imagination. And all of this seems to require space and time as forms of sensibility, or to require at least *some* forms of sensibility which will present us with sensory data as a manifold.

Our hypothetical subject with an intellectual intuition, however, does not *receive* sensory data at all, and certainly not through the forms of space and time. For this reason there is nothing like "our" activity of synthesis which such a being would need to perform. So is the consciousness of such a being a unity, and could it be this unity of its consciousness which constitutes its relation to an object? To this question we can give no answer because talking about the unity of consciousness involves the question of the role of concepts in our experience, and it is precisely

---

[14]Kant remarks in the Transcendental Aesthetic that God's knowledge must consist entirely of intuition "and not thought, which always involves limitations" (B17). He also tells us on the same page that it is possible that "all finite, thinking beings necessarily agree with man in this respect," i.e., in respect of having space and time as forms of intuition.

his thought about concepts which leads Kant into his coherence theory of knowledge. A being with an intuitive understanding presumably does not have concepts at all—it does not need them—and so the whole notion of coherence or necessary connection would not apply to the consciousness of such a being.

As a final speculation, however, I will suggest that there may be one way in which Kant's coherence view of consciousness does make its presence felt even in this section of the *Critique of Pure Reason*. This is in Kant's conviction that to be is to be the object of some sort of intuition. This belief of Kant does not appear to rest on the kind of psychological arguments which lead Berkeley to his doctrine of *esse est percipi*. Rather, it may be based on Kant's conception of what "objectively real," "how things are in their own nature," and similar expressions mean to *us*, and how the concepts which are involved in these expressions relate to *our* experience. These considerations lead Kant into his deepest form of idealism, his view that we can have no conception of a totally non-mental reality and that therefore the thing in itself, if unknown to us, must be known by some other subject of experience. All of this, however, cannot become clear without an examination of this other, necessary-connection view of consciousness which Kant holds along with his correspondence view.

Kant's Coherence Theory of Consciousness

Intuitions and Concepts

The coherence theory of consciousness in Kant is harder to understand and to explain than is his correspondence theory, which is closer to our ordinary conceptions of consciousness and knowledge. Yet this coherence view is at the heart of the most profound, revolutionary part of Kant's philosophy. It represents Kant's deepest analysis of the relation of consciousness to its object in the sense that is the theory to which Kant adheres when he is focusing his attention on precisely this question. Unlike the correspondence view, which is not formally presented anywhere but is simply assumed throughout the *Critique*, the necessary-connection view is given some very explicit argumentation. Before we begin to examine the relevant passages, however, we need to remind ourselves of those Kantian doctrines which form their background.

The basic doctrine here, which is not essential to the correspondence view of consciousness but is required even to state the coherence view, is Kant's contrast between intuitions and concepts. This contrast is first expressed clearly by Kant at the very beginning of his Transcendental Logic and is stated again much later at the end of this section of the *Critique*, where Kant attacks both Locke and Leibniz for failing to make this distinction adequately (A271).[15] Sensory data, or "empirical intuitions" in Kant's terminology, constitute the sensational element in experience. All of it is given to the subject at least in temporal form because time is for Kant the form of inner sense, and some it is in spatial form as well through the form of outer sense. Both time and space are, for Kant, subject-imposed forms which result in the sensational aspect of consciousness being "given" to the subject in spatio-temporal guise.

But for Kant there could be no conscious experience which consisted only of such sensory data, even as given through the forms of space and time. Such a supposed experience, consisting of intuition without thought, would be "for us as good as nothing" (A111), "merely a blind play of representations, less even than a dream" (A112). What is required in addition are concepts; more specifically, that mental activity is required which is called the "use" of concepts or the "application" of concepts to sensory data. Now it is very difficult to get an intelligible account from either Kant or his commentators of exactly what this mental activity amounts to. The official story is that this is the activity of (transcendental) synthesis, whereby the separate parts of the sensory manifold are combined into a single consciousness of an apparent space-time world through those particular functions or rules of synthesis called the categories. This doctrine of conceptual activity or synthesis is so difficult, however, that it is hard for the commentator to be sure that he is truly explaining Kant's theory rather than just *saying* what Kant says in slightly different terminology.

---

[15]The distinction between intuitions and concepts is recognized by the commentators as a crucial Kantian insight. Clear statements of this in the recent literature are in John Bennett's *Kant's Dialectic* (Cambridge: Cambridge University Press, 1974) 9-39, and in Strawson's *The Bounds of Sense*, 20-21 and 49. One weakness in Strawson's account of this distinction is that he never tells us what exactly, either in Kant's view or his own, it is which concepts *do* or what difference they make in experience. This is no doubt due to Strawson's refusal to involve himself in the details of Kant's transcendental psychology, but it surely results in something important being left out of Kant's philosophy, in his account of it.

The following points are reasonably clear about Kant's doctrine of concepts. For Kant a concept is fundamentally different from any sensory datum, whether vivid or unvivid; a concept is not simply a weak or faded impression as Hume claims. Rather, concepts are abilities of the mind to handle sensory data in various way. Furthermore, we know that in Kant's view conceptual activity is crucial in making the subject's consciousness a unity. Without this activity and the unity which it produces, it would mean nothing to say that two different items of sensation—a visual impression of red and a particular auditory impression, for example—were parts of the same conscious experience. The use of concepts is also necessary to the subject's awareness of himself as the subject of his consciousness. In what may be the most obscure of all of Kant's doctrines, that of the transcendental unity of apperception, Kant attempts to prove this connection between conceptual activity and self-consciousness. Finally, concepts are necessary for the intentionality of consciousness, for consciousness to be an awareness or thought "of" something. It is this latter Kantian insight which renders the correspondence view of consciousness inadequate and leads Kant into the coherence or necessary-connection doctrine. If we assume that subject and object are two distinct entities and that, by whatever relationship, the object "affects" the subject to produce sensory data which are literally within the subject, we will be no closer to understanding this most mysterious fact about consciousness—the fact that it is "of" something. Even if the sensory data in the mind of the subject exactly resembled some external object which caused them (if we can make any sense of the notion of resemblance here), this similarity between data and object would not make this effect "of" its cause in the sense in which my consciousness is "of" a real world.[16] For the latter to obtain, these sensory data must be regarded by the subject as constituting an awareness of an object, and this regarding or interpreting of the data surely requires some sort of mental activity on the part of the subject over and above the mere occurrence of events or states within the subject. Pursuing this line of thought will take us into Kant's doctrine of synthesis. However, we may wish to interpret this doctrine and

---

[16]Karl Ameriks makes this point in "Kantian Idealism Today." He argues that to say simply that the object of awareness causes or produces a representation in the subject "is insufficient to explain the peculiarity of *epistemic* representation as such" (330).

whatever mistakes or confusions we may attribute to Kant here, it seems clear that this theory is quite a fundamental part of Kant's philosophy and cannot be detached from it as easily as some recent commentators have supposed.

Taking an overview of all of this, we can regard Kant's philosophy as the grandest of all philosophical enterprises. Kant may be viewed as attempting to answer Descartes's question about the external reference of consciousness ("How do I know that my consciousness is *of* a real world?") along with Hume's question about the unity of consciousness ("What is it which makes different 'perceptions' part of the same mind or the same consciousness?"). He will answer both of these questions with a single theory of consciousness and of mental activity which will show the link between the unity of consciousness, self-awareness, and consciousness being "of an object." The theory which will accomplish all of this will have as a very important ingredient Kant's distinction between intuitions and concepts as fundamentally different, but equally essential, components of our experience. Furthermore, this theory when developed fully will involve a break with the correspondence view of knowledge. With the heroic grandiosity of Kant's ambitions, plus his apparent assurance that he has realized them all, plus the extreme, cryptic difficulty of the text, it is no wonder that Kant's philosophy has provided endless material for scholarly exegesis.

Although Kant insists on the distinction between intuitions and concepts, he insists equally emphatically that concepts have meaning, i.e., use, only with reference to sensory data. We might draw the Kantian distinction between pure concepts and empirical concepts by saying that empirical concepts depend for their usefulness upon certain specific sensory data. I could not recognize something as being red, or a elephant, if certain intuitions did not present themselves to me. These concepts are not necessary to my having experience because in the absence of these particular sensory data I might have other data to which I applied other concepts. By contrast, pure concepts or categories are those which, Kant claims, must be applied to any sensory data whatsoever. They are necessary conditions of experience in that they are required for the synthesis of sensory data into a single consciousness and for its reference outward as an awareness of some real world. But even though the pure concepts are not tied to specific kinds of sensory data, they clearly require *some* data; without this they are "empty" and could not give us awareness or experience of anything at all.

Concepts and Reality

In tracing out the implications of the dependence of concepts upon intuitions, Kant must at some point have realized the following: that we do have the concept of "real" or "objective reality" or "how things are in their own nature," and that this concept, like any other, is in some sense in the mind of the subject. It is an ability of the subject to deal with sensory data. If we examine this concept of "objectively real" and how it functions in our experience, we may shed light on the exegetical question of what function Kant thinks this concept must perform in the mind of any conscious being. This will lead us, in turn, into Kant's view of the nature of concepts and conceptual activity generally. All of this will be very relevant to Kant's coherence theory of the relation of consciousness to its object and, finally, to the question of what sort of idealism Kant espouses.

When we attempt to explicate our concept of "objectively real," it is useful to ask what this concept contrasts with, that is, to ask what we mean when we say that something is *not* real. In this connection John Austin has argued that there can be no one concept or idea which is conveyed by "real" precisely because there are so many different terms which can be contrasted with it. Austin infers from this that what "real" means on any occasion of its use depends upon what the opposite of real is taken to be (as "dyed," "decoy," "toy," "dummy," and so on.)[17] This is perhaps true, but we could nevertheless argue that the basic contrast here, which gives "objectively real" its root meaning to any subject of experience, is the contrast with how things appear to that subject given the subject's own nature as an individual mind and his particular place in the world. Indeed, this conception of how things really are will arise for me as soon as I have a conception of myself as an individual person and as forming a very small part of a wider world. I will then have an idea of my own perspective on this world which, because of the finite, limited nature of myself, is also finite and limited; and I will also have an idea of that portion of the world which falls outside of my perspective. Coming to know (more about) how things really are in their own

---

[17]John Austin, *Sense and Sensibilia* (New York: Oxford University Press, 1964) 62-83.

intrinsic nature will involve the correction or improvement of this perspective.

A very great deal of this broadening of my view of things will result simply from my interactions with other human beings. We can all to some extent pool our experience so that each of us can add the experience of others to his own limited experience of the world. In addition, modern science enables us to view things in a wider context in a variety of ways. Spatially, a thing has a hidden micro-structure plus a set of relationships with other objects and temporally, it has a past and a future. We gain a better understanding of what the thing in question really is when we are able to widen our view to include these aspects of it. And, of course, it is not just our spatial and temporal perspective on things which is limited; our sensory modalities themselves may give us an incomplete or distorted awareness even of the objects of ordinary perception. With scientific instruments we may attempt to compensate for all of this. Finally, we may recognize that our ways of thinking about the world may be capable of improvement so as to get us closer to thinking of the world as it really is. When we claim to have discovered that an object or event A is, in its own intrinsic nature, actually a B, we are attempting to move in the direction from appearance to reality. We claim that our conception of "B" tells us more about what or how the thing in question is than "A" did. In all of this progress we must have an antecedent conception that things do have an intrinsic nature in themselves, and this conception must serve as a kind of goal of our inquiries.[18]

This connection between our conception of reality and our conception of a corrected or "broadened" or otherwise improved perspective is urged by Strawson in *The Bounds of Sense*.[19] Strawson argues that when we contrast the notion of reality to that of appearance, we conceive of reality as that which we would apprehend (more of) if our perspective on the world did not have the various limitations which it has. Strawson intends this as a criticism of Kant, but the criticism in fact applies only to Kant's

---

[18] An excellent discussion of the conceptual contrast between appearance and reality is contained in Thomas Nagel's article, "Subjective and Objective," in *Mortal Questions* (Cambridge: Cambridge University Press, 1979) 196-213, and is developed at much greater length in his book *The View from Nowhere* (New York: Oxford University Press, 1986).

[19] Strawson, *Bounds of Sense*, 250-55.

correspondence view of consciousness. If we take this correspondence view of the relation of consciousness to its object and adopt Kant's own extreme version of his Copernican Revolution, and take the subject of experience to be the individual person, the Kantian view would be that reality is the thing in itself and that the space-time world, as "only" appearance, is in some sense *un*real. This conception of reality would, of course, be a conception of something to which we could never get any closer by any possible improvement in our epistemic situation and hence would be subject to Strawson's criticism.

But even though Kant's correspondence view of consciousness, along with his Copernican Revolution, would seem to imply this application of the term "reality" to the intrinsically unknowable thing in itself, I have pointed out that Kant himself, unlike most of this commentators, is quite hesitant to use the term in this way. The reason is that Kant also holds the coherence view of "of an object." With his theory of concepts and their relation to experience, he sees that our concept of objective reality, if "reality" *means* anything to us, must apply within the world of our experience. All of this results in perhaps the deepest internal strain in the entire Kantian philosophy. Taking the correspondence view of consciousness, Kant labels the entire space-time world "appearance." If reality is contrasted with appearance, as it normally is, then the thing in itself will constitute reality. But Kant also holds the coherence or necessary-connection view, which is linked to his idea of what concepts are and how they function in experience. When he is subscribing to this view of the relation of consciousness to its object, his position is that the contrast between objective reality (how things are in their own nature) and whatever is supposed to contrast with it (i.e., appearance) must be drawn within experience and hence must apply within the space-time world rather than between this world and something else. Therefore, when Kant is espousing his coherence view with this latter sort of contrast between appearance and reality, Strawson's criticism of him is invalid; for in this strand of his thinking Kant would agree with Strawson that reality is what we can and do obtain increasing knowledge of with improvements in our perception and thought.

The Transcendental Object

Kant's two different views of what it means to say that consciousness is "of an object" and the two altogether different ways of handling the contrast between appearance and reality come together in his doctrine of the transcendental object or "object in general = X." This is by all accounts one of the more difficult of Kantian doctrines and has received considerable attention in the literature. Kemp Smith characterizes this doctrine as "pre-Critical" and says that the transcendental object is simply "the thing in itself, regarded as the object of our representations."[20] According to Kemp Smith, all of the passages in which Kant speaks of the transcendental object were written at a time when Kant believed that we can have knowledge of the thing in itself and then were carelessly (*very* carelessly) inserted into the *Critique* when this work was being prepared for publication. I agree with Paton that it is difficult to believe that the first *Critique* is that much of a patchwork, especially since, as I will argue, a better interpretation of the transcendental object can be given. (Remarkably, neither Strawson's nor Bennett's commentary on the *Critique of Pure Reason* contains any reference to the transcendental object.)

In the text of the first *Critique* there are passages in which the expression, "transcendental object," is used in connection with the correspondence view of consciousness, and here it refers to the thing in itself. There are other passages, however, especially in the first edition version of the Transcendental Deduction, in which this expression clearly does not refer to the thing in itself, and here an entirely different view of consciousness is being presented. Let me first state this view and then present the textual evidence for it.

Kant believes that when the mind is passively given a manifold of sensory data under the forms of space and time, it then actively ties together or synthesizes these data into a single conscious experience. Furthermore, the mind does this not haphazardly but according to certain fixed rules. These rules, or ways in which intuitions are tied together, are called by Kant the pure concepts or categories; they result in certain features of our experience, and thus also features of the world as it appears to us, which Kant believes are a priori necessary in the sense of being required for any ("human") experience to occur at all. Kant has great confidence in his ability to identify all of these necessary ways of combining sensory data into experience, and his assurance here rests partly on his conviction that this faculty of combination, the understanding, is an "absolute unity" and that the pure concepts "must

---

[20]Kemp Smith, *Commentary*, 204.

therefore be connected with each other according to one concept or idea" (A67). This "one concept" is our concept of the transcendental object. It is the mind's ability for synthesis as such, and this general capacity is realized in those specific ways of combining intuitions which are the categories. As Kant says, the categories "only serve to determine the transcendental object, which is the concept of something in general, through that which is given in sensibility" (A251).

Kant's concept of "something in general" is, I maintain, just our conception of reality per se—what there actually is or what our awareness is *of* prior to any contrast between this object of our awareness "as it appears" versus "as it is in itself." We must not fail to see the radical nature of Kant's doctrine here. When he develops his account of the transcendental object, Kant is taking Descartes's question, "How do I know that my consciousness is of an object?," very seriously. But he is looking at this question from within the mind of the questioning subject, and he concludes that the only difference to me as subject between the sensory data in my mind being only properties of myself and their constituting an awareness of an external reality lies in the relations among these representations themselves. If my sensory data, my intuitions, are combined in the "categorial" ways into a single consciousness, this "combinedness" is just what it *means*, all that it *can* mean to me, the subject of experience, for my consciousness to be of an object. So it is by means of this activity of synthesis that my sensory data become an awareness of an external reality; but this external reality and the status of my consciousness as being "of" this reality are nothing more than the unity of my consciousness itself via the categories.

A Disagreement with Strawson

Here I must disagree with Strawson, who I believe distorts Kant's views in his eagerness to dissociate Kant and himself from Descartes. Strawson tells us that Kant rejects problematic idealism, which Strawson defines as the doctrine that we are not directly aware of an objective world but rather only of the "private data of individual consciousness" and that we must "justify our belief in the objective world by working outward, as it were" from our own states of consciousness.[21] According to Strawson, Kant's theory of experience involves a radical rejection of

---

[21]Strawson, *Bounds of Sense*, 19.

the Cartesian starting point, of the view that I am initially certain only of my own states of mind and that something further is needed in order for me to know of anything beyond this. Yet the text shows that Kant is not as far from Descartes as Strawson asserts. The one place in the first *Critique* where Kant explicitly argues against Descartes's problematic idealism is in the fourth Paralogism of the first edition. Here Kant does indeed reject Descartes's view that my knowledge of physical objects is doubtful because I can be aware only of my own representations; but he overcomes this doubt by *reducing* physical objects to representations:

> There can be no question that I am conscious of my representations; these representations and I myself, who have the representations, therefore exist. External objects (bodies), however, are mere appearances, and are therefore nothing but a species of my representations, the objects of which are something only through these representations. (A370)

Of course, it is too simple to call Kant just a phenomenalist, one who reduces the object of consciousness to consciousness itself. As I have argued, Kant does subscribe to a correspondence theory of consciousness in the two different versions which I have described. Throughout this strand of his thinking, Kant is indeed rejecting the Cartesian starting point; but it should be emphasized that he is not rejecting it because of any argument. He simply assumes what Descartes doubts and then goes on to tell a further story about how this object of our awareness must "affect" and appear to us. When he does present an argument about how I can know that there is any object of my consciousness at all, he drops the correspondence view and gives us instead the coherence view of consciousness according to which this "object" is only the unity, via the categories, of this consciousness itself. Strawson does not deal with this latter theory, or recognize the extent of its Cartesian basis, because of his disdain for Kant's transcendental psychology.

The Concept of External Reality and Kant's Coherence Theory

Before we look at the details of the coherence theory of consciousness as Kant develops this theory in the text of the *Critique*, we may consider some of its major implications. The first is that under this doctrine there will be no place for an unknowable thing in itself. If the mind literally determines its object through the synthetic activities of the understanding, then this "object" of consciousness will exist precisely as known; indeed, its *being* and its *being known* will be identical, and there will be no room for any intrinsically unknowable "side" to it. Kant's inclination in the section on Phenomena and Noumena to say that the unknowable (to us) thing in itself must be known by some other kind of intuition may therefore be an instance of his coherence theory of consciousness being grafted onto his correspondence view.

Another implication of the coherence doctrine is that the space-time world will be unequivocally real. If the concept of the transcendental object is just the mind's concept of external reality per se (the concept of "what my awareness is *of*"), and if the categories are simply specific determinations of this overall concept or mental ability, and if the categories impose certain essential features upon the phenomenal world of our experience, then we can understand Kant's indignation at the idea that his philosophy might be equated with that of Berkeley. Kant attributed to Berkeley the doctrine that the physical world is in some fairly strong sense unreal, such that "all knowledge through the senses and experience is nothing but sheer illusion."[22] He could claim in response that his philosophy is the direct opposite of Berkeley's on this point. Kant could say that he is not only telling us that the space-time world is real but that he is the first philosopher to explain to us exactly *how* it is real. His list of categories, he could say, and his account of how the categories function in experience constitute an explication of our concept of "objectively real." Therefore, the physical world is indeed real because certain features of this world, which no object of our awareness could lack, constitute what "real" *means*.

Yet although Kant can say that according to his philosophy the space-time world is as real as we have always believed it to be, he must make the additional point that the very reality of this world is thought into it by the knowing subject. For the peculiar fact about consciousness, that it is of an object, is just the unity or synthesis of sensory data into a single conscious experience; and the realness of this "object" which

---

[22] Kant, *Prolegomena*, 374 in the Academy edition. This is, of course, highly questionable as an interpretation of Berkeley. For interesting treatments of the question of how much Kant actually knew about the philosophy of Berkeley, see Colin Turbayne's "Kant's Relation to Berkeley," *Philosophical Quarterly* 5 (1955): 225-44; Margaret Wilson's "Kant and the Dogmatic Idealism of Berkeley," *Journal of the History of Philosophy* 9 (1971): 459-75; and Henry Allison's "Kant's Critique of Berkeley," *Journal of the History of Philosophy* 11 (1973): 43-63.

consciousness is "of" consists of the various categorial ways in which sensory data are combined into a single consciousness. And finally, of course, this entire activity of combination comes from within the subject rather than being imposed from without.

Textual Statements of Kant's Coherence Theory

At this point we should have a look at the textual basis in the first *Critique* for this interpretation of Kant. The coherence theory is so much at variance with what Kant says elsewhere, especially about the thing in itself, and it is in some ways so bizarre in its own right, that one might wonder whether Kant actually maintains such a position. It turns out, however, that there is considerable explicit argumentation for this theory in the body of the *Critique*. In this respect it is in contrast to the correspondence theory, which is never explicitly argued for or even stated in much detail. The correspondence theory is implied in the "language of appearing" and also in the "language of appearance" where the thing in itself is seen as the cause of representations. There is a great deal of this language in the Transcendental Aesthetic, yet it is by no means found only here but is scattered throughout the first *Critique*. The coherence theory, on the other hand, is explicitly argued for, both in the Transcendental Deduction (most clearly in the first edition) and also in a section of the second Analogy of Experience. This part of the Second Analogy looks, in fact, as though it had been lifted out of the first edition Transcendental Deduction. The coherence theory is also mentioned and implied elsewhere in the *Critique*, but these are the only passages which warrant detailed exegesis.

Transcendental Deduction, First Edition

At A104 Kant asks what we can mean by the expression, "object of representations." Our immediate awareness is only of appearances, or "sensible representations," which cannot be taken as things existing apart from our consciousness of them. So what can we mean when we say that these immediate objects of consciousness, these sensible representations, are themselves "of" some object? We must think of this object initially, Kant says, only as "something in general = X"; we think of it in a neutral way as nothing more than that (whatever it is) which our consciousness is *of*. But what is expressed by this "of"-relationship? Kant's view is that it must contain an element of necessity: "The object is viewed as that which prevents our modes of knowledge from being haphazard or arbitrary, and which determines them a priori in some definite fashion." Furthermore, a necessary condition of my states of mind together constituting an awareness *of* something is that they "agree with one another" in certain ways.

All of this is acceptable so far. I do indeed have this notion that my consciousness is "of" some object or real world. And I do at very least think of this object of my consciousness as being what determines my consciousness to be the way it is. We need not have any specifically causal conception of the relation between our awareness and its object, and still less do we need to speak of a resemblance between consciousness and object; we need only say that if my awareness is "of an object," then the object must in some way necessitate the fact that my consciousness is the way it is. Furthermore, a degree of unity or coherence in my consciousness is certainly a necessary condition of my thinking that my consciousness is an awareness *of* something. Humean vividness of sensory data would not suffice here—if my consciousness were incoherent, no amount of force or vivacity of my individual sensory data could make me suppose that I was aware of a real world. On the other hand, even weak perceptions might constitute an awareness of some real object if they had sufficient coherence with one another.

Slightly later in the text, at A105 Kant tells us that we "have to deal" only with the multiplicity of our own mental states and that, therefore, any object which corresponds to them is "nothing" to us. He infers from this fact that the unity or coherence of consciousness which this object "makes necessary" (i.e., which the consciousness must have if it is to be "of an object") can be only "the formal unity of consciousness in the synthesis of the manifold of representations," and that therefore "it is only when we have thus produced synthetic unity in the manifold of intuition that we are in a position to say that we know the object." It is crucial here that Kant speaks of "we," the knowing subject, having produced this unity. His view is that it is the subject himself, through those processes which cannot be an object of experience because they are preconditions of experience, who literally creates the required unity and coherence in his consciousness such that he can regard his consciousness as being of an object. And Kant is not saying that the subject is *wrong* in regarding his awareness as being "of a real world," because this unity of the subject's consciousness, however it arises, is all that "of a real world" can possibly *mean* for *any* subject of experience. For Kant says that the concept of this "unity of rule" whereby the multiplicity of my mental states is "determined," i.e., tied together into a single consciousness, simply *is* my representation of the "object = X" which I regard as the object of my consciousness.

After speaking of apperception and arguing for a link between the subject's awareness of himself and those synthetic activities which make his consciousness to be "of an object," Kant returns in A109 to "our concept of an object in general." He tells us again that all that is "given to us immediately" are appearances, which Kant, as before, regards as states of mind of the subject. He then says that these representations "have their object," are *of* an external reality, and he describes this reality as "an object which cannot itself be intuited by us, and which may, therefore, be named the non-empirical, that is, transcendental object = X."

Now it is rather strange to define the transcendental object as the object of consciousness and then to say that this object "cannot itself be intuited by us." For if it cannot be intuited, it cannot be known, and surely the *object* of consciousness is just that thing, whatever it is, which *is* known. What we must have here is a case of Kant entwining his correspondence and his coherence theories of knowledge in the same passage. According to the correspondence view, knowledge involves a relation of the subject to an independent object which, because of the subject's contribution to experience, cannot be known as it is in itself but only as it appears. Hence the doctrine of the thing in itself. According to the coherence theory, knowledge involves a unity of representations, a unity which is thought into experience by the mind itself. Hence we have the transcendental object *rather than* the "object" which cannot be known as it is in itself. When Kant makes the amazing statement that the object of knowledge cannot be known, he must be saying that from the subject's point of view (from which standpoint the coherence theory of "of an object" is developed) an object "outside of my representations" envisioned as merely the cause of my representations could not be intuited or known and hence would be "nothing to me." We will see that in the second edition Deduction Kant takes a more consistent view of the object of awareness.

The very next paragraph (A109-110) contains Kant's clearest statement of his coherence view of knowledge. The concept of the transcendental object, Kant says, "throughout all our knowledge is always one and the same." This concept "contains no determinate intuition" and is what "can alone confer upon all our empirical concepts in general relation to an object, that is, objective reality." Because there is no specific intuition, or sensory datum, which is required by our concept of the transcendental object, the concept

> therefore refers only to that unity which must be met with in any manifold of knowledge which stands in relation to an object. This relation is nothing but the necessary unity of consciousness, and therefore of the synthesis of the manifold, through a common function of the mind.

This unity is "necessary a priori," a fact which implies for Kant that it is imposed from within by the mind itself. And Kant finally tells us that "the relation to a transcendental object, that is, the objective reality of our empirical knowledge," rests on the requirement that representations, if "through them objects are to be given us," must conform to the mind-imposed requirements for the unity of these mental states in a single consciousness experience.

All of this squares with my earlier contentions about Kant's coherence view of consciousness. When he puts himself in Descartes's philosophical position and raises doubts about the external reference of his own consciousness, Kant sees that even if the subject's states of consciousness were caused in him by external things and even if there were whatever sort of correspondence one wished between states of mind and objects in the world, this correspondence would not suffice to give the subject himself the idea of a real world or the idea of his representations as being *of* a real world. Nor would it suffice to give the subject a conception of himself as the single subject of his states of mind. For both self-awareness and other-awareness, something more is required beyond simply the existence or occurrence of sensations in the mind of the subject, whether these sensory data are produced from without or not. Kant believes that he can account for both of these additional factors at once through his theory of concepts. If a concept is an ability of the mind to handle sensory data and if the "pure" concepts are abilities to unite disparate data into one conscious experience, then surely this concept of the transcendental object is simply the mind's capacity for synthesis as such. As a concept *of* something, it is the subject's idea of "what there really is," that external reality to which he conceives his consciousness to be related. This concept requires no *specific* sensory data because it is the subject's ability to unify *whatever* data are presented to him. Likewise, my concept of a real world and my idea that my consciousness is *of* a real world do not tell me in advance anything about what sorts of sensory data I will be presented with. They rather tell me only that these data will have certain sorts of unity and coherence (or "necessary connection") with one another. In fact, of course, Kant believes that a much more detailed story than this can be told about what sorts of coherence these representations must have. This story is Kant's account of how the categories function in experience to tie representations together and at the same time "project" them outward as a single awareness of a real world. But if these sensory data are so united in a single consciousness, then, Kant believes, the resulting state of mind is necessarily an awareness of a real world; for this unity of consciousness is all that "of a real world" can possibly *mean* to the knowing subject.

Immediately after this account of the transcendental object there is a passage (A110) which was discussed above (32) about the "one single experience in which all perceptions are represented as in thoroughgoing and orderly connection." Kant relates this "single experience" to the fact that "there is only one space and one time in which all modes of appearance and all relations of being or not being occur." He tells us that "When we speak of different experiences, we can refer only to the various perceptions, all of which, as such, belong to one and the same general experience." This is the first passage in the *Critique of Pure Reason* which could be taken to indicate that the Kantian subject of experience is not to be identified with the individual human person. As I argued earlier, however, this passage does not need to be so interpreted, and if Kant intended here to argue for a world-soul or universal consciousness encompassing the phenomenal world, surely he would have made this more explicit.

Yet there may be something of interest going on here regarding the Kantian subject of experience. If we adopt Kant's coherence view of consciousness, the unity of the phenomenal world which I apprehend is reducible to the "necessary unity" of my representations in a single consciousness. But if each subject is an entity separate from all other subjects, then there will not be one objective world which contains all of these subjects. And Kant himself would reject any attempt to create a single world just by calling the plurality of subjects "one totality." For as early as his *Inaugural Dissertation*, Kant says in criticism of Leibnitz that monads, or whatever ultimate parts of things there are, must have a real physical (causal) interaction rather than just a "virtual" interaction through a pre-established harmony. This is necessary because otherwise these individual items, these monads, would not form a genuine whole; there would be not one world but many. According to Robert Paul Wolff, this thesis becomes the doctrine in the first *Critique* that "all objects of experience must stand in thoroughgoing community, since whatever cannot be connected with all other contents of consciousness in a unity would simply not enter consciousness, and hence be as nothing to me."[23] Now if Kant's coherence view of the outward reference of consciousness is true and if the subject of experience is the individual person, then from the point of view of each of these monadic entities, the idea of there being *other* centers of consciousness as fellow inhabitants of "my" world will be meaningless; such entities will be "nothing to me." If other minds are to be "something" to me, we must have one phenomenal world *containing* my own mind plus others, and these individual minds must, it would seem, themselves be in causal relation to one another. All of this means that if Kant adheres to his coherence theory of consciousness, he will be pushed in the direction of saying that there is "one single experience" to which all of the particular experiences of different individuals somehow belong. This, in turn will lead Kant toward a doctrine of an all-encompassing Mind or Soul as the source of the unity and intelligibility of the world.

In the remainder of the first edition Deduction Kant introduces the notion of the categories as "conditions of thought in a possible experience" and says that they are "fundamental concepts by which we think objects in general." This latter remark supports my contention that the categories together constitute the concept of the transcendental object, or that objective reality which I regard my consciousness as being "of." Kant also tells us more about the activity of synthesis and about apperception—that kind of self-awareness which is inseparable from synthesis and hence also inseparable from my awareness of my representations as being of a real world. It might be thought that this doctrine of ("transcendental") self-awareness could have some bearing upon our question of who is the Kantian subject and also on the matter of how this question is affected by Kant's coherence theory of consciousness. I cannot see, however, that there is much that we can infer from Kant's doctrine of apperception regarding these questions. There may be some weighty implications which simply escape me since Kant's view of self-consciousness is (to me) one of the most obscure parts of the entire *Critique*. As I have pointed out, however, (see above, 41) Kant does

---

[23]Wolff, *Kant's Theory*, 14.

The Relation of Consciousness to Its Object 75

argue at length in the Paralogisms that the "I think," whatever it is, does not contain any intuition, hence cannot be the object of any concept, and hence cannot be used to prove the existence of a persisting Cartesian ego, even as appearance. This being the case, it would seem equally unlikely that we could squeeze out of the "I think" anything regarding any other kind of individual ego or collective Ego.

Transcendental Deduction, Second Edition

The theory of consciousness which Kant presents in his second edition version of the Transcendental Deduction is, I think, largely unchanged from what we find in the first edition. This occurs in spite of the disappearance of the term "transcendental object" in the second edition, a fact which Kemp Smith regards as evidence of a fundamental shift in doctrine. If by "transcendental object" Kant just meant "thing in itself," as Kemp Smith asserts, then there would indeed be a different view of consciousness put forward in the two editions. But if the concept of this object is rather the unity which the mind thinks into experience and is the concept of the external reality generally which is the object of consciousness, then the two editions contain pretty much the same doctrine. This raises the question, however, of why Kant decided to drop the use of "transcendental object." My only suggestion is that Kant may have realized that he had a conflict between his correspondence and his coherence theories of consciousness, or at least that there was *some* sort of tension in what he meant by "of an object" and that this tension was somehow involved in his doctrine of the transcendental object. Rather than truly coming to grips with this problem in his philosophy, however, Kant may have taken the easier course of simply dropping the expression, "transcendental object."

Early in the second edition Deduction (B131), Kant says that we have a concept of "the unity of the manifold" of given sensory data. This looks very much like the concept of the transcendental object since Kant says that this concept of unity "precedes a priori all concepts of combination" (categories). After a section on apperception, we find at B137 a paragraph in which Kant's coherence theory of the outward reference of consciousness is expressed as clearly as Kant expresses it anywhere. He says that the understanding, the mind's capacity for synthesis, is the faculty of knowledge. Knowledge, in turn, "consists in the determinate relations of given representations to an object." The object of consciousness, Kant says, is "that in the concept of which the manifold of a given intuition is united." This expression, which is as awkward in its original German as it is in English, again calls to mind the transcendental object of the A Deduction. The subject has a concept of the object of his consciousness simply qua object, as whatever it is which his consciousness is *of,* and it is "in" this concept—by means of this ability of synthesis generally—that any given "manifold" or multiplicity of intuition is brought together in a single consciousness. This is exactly Kant's doctrine of the transcendental object with only the expression deleted. It is by being brought together in one consciousness that intuitions—sensory data—come to have their outward reference because this necessary unity just *is* the reference of these data to an external reality: "Consequently, it is the unity of consciousness that alone constitutes the relation of representations to an object, and therefore their objective validity, and the fact that they are modes of knowledge" (B137).

But however clear may be Kant's commitment to this coherence view of knowledge, Kant continues to hold a correspondence view as well. Perhaps the strongest indication of this is in B146. Here, after characterizing a category as the concept "through which an object in general is thought," he adds that it is through intuition that this same object is "given." Kant does not appear to see that there are two altogether different views of the external reference of consciousness embodied in this simple characterization of the difference between intuitions and concepts. The coherence theory tells us that it is by thought, the activity of the understanding, that the "object in general" comes into being, for this object in general, this "whatever my consciousness is *of,*" is a function of the unity of sensory data in one consciousness. But to say that this very same object is also "given" in intuition is now to tell us something quite different. Here the object of awareness is seen as something which exists independently of the subject and his mental activities. It is something which is "given" to the subject through "affecting" the faculty of sensibility to "produce" intuitions. Telling this story, Kant can then go on to say that because of the distorting nature of our sensibility, this object does not appear to us as it is in its own nature, but rather appears as a spatio-temporal world. But even so, this object with that inherent nature which makes it a thing in itself is quite independent of the subject, unlike the transcendental object which is put into experience by thought.

There would seem to be quite a serious problem for Kant's theory of knowledge in his characterization of the same object of knowledge as both "given" and "thought." Kant holds that intuition and thought are both essential components of experience, yet he has one theory of the external reference of consciousness connected with his view of intuition and quite another connected with his view of thought. The fact that these two theories are not only different but incompatible bodes ill for the prospect of arriving at an acceptable "Kantian" theory through any simple modification of what we find in the first *Critique*.

The Second Analogy of Experience

The one remaining part of the *Critique of Pure Reason* in which the question of the outward reference of consciousness is discussed in any detail is a portion of the second Analogy of Experience. All of Kant's Analogies, and especially the second, have received an enormous amount of attention in the literature on Kant; here I will try to focus only on what is relevant to our immediate question. What we find in the second Analogy, as in the Transcendental Deduction, is the "necessary connection" view of the outward reference of consciousness. Indeed, this necessary synthesis of intuitions in a single consciousness becomes in Kant's arguments the necessary (causal) connection of things in the phenomenal world. Furthermore, we can see in the second Analogy more clearly than elsewhere the impact upon one another of our questions about the status of the Kantian subject and about the outward reference of consciousness. One thing that makes this section so difficult, I suggest, is that Kant himself sees the conflict between what he wants to say about consciousness and what he would like to say about a public phenomenal world. His convoluted arguments in this section represent in part his unsuccessful attempts to resolve this conflict.

In the third paragraph of his second Analogy (A189-190—this is the first paragraph in the A edition), Kant reminds us that the occurrence of the manifold of representations in the mind is always successive. The occurrence of this succession, however, does not tell the subject whether or not there is also a successive alteration in that external state of affairs which is the object of these representations. The distinguishing of these two kinds of succession then leads Kant into an enquiry about what exactly is meant by "object of representations." He tells us that the representations in the mind of the subject, as long as the subject is conscious of these states of mind, may be entitled objects. This sort of object of awareness, these "appearances, in so far as they are objects of consciousness simply in virtue of being representations," are like

Berkeleyan ideas in that they are nothing apart from their apprehension by the subject. (This passage, incidentally, is further evidence against Strawson's assertion of a radical difference between Kant and Descartes with regard to the notion of the veil of consciousness. Kant's argument in proof of an external world is certainly different from that of Descartes, but his starting point, the view that I am immediately aware of only my own states of mind, seems to be thoroughly Cartesian.)

Yet these representations, Kant tells us, in addition to being states of myself which are objects of my consciousness, are also said to "stand for" (*bezeichnen*) an object, and we must ask what is meant by "object" in this latter sense. We regard as the objects of our consciousness what Kant terms appearances, physical entities and events in space and time. Now let us suppose that these are things in themselves, in the sense of existing and having the nature which they have totally independent of the subject and his mental activities. In this case, Kant says, "since we have to deal solely with our representations," we could never infer from the order of these representations anything about the order of things in the space-time world. In fact, of course, the phenomenal world is not a thing in itself, and this is what allows us to have knowledge of it on the basis of our representations.

At this point Kant is forced to draw a distinction where there seems to be none to be drawn. He must say that although appearances (objects and events in the physical world) are not things in themselves and thus in *some* sense are not anything over and above the successive states of mind in the knowing subject, in some *other* sense they *are* something apart from mental representations. To illustrate the relation between appearances and states of mind, Kant gives the example of the house "which stands before me." Here the order of representations in my mind is successive as I survey the house, but "no one will grant" that the parts of the house itself exist one after the other. (Notice that the subject of experience here must be the individual person. A cosmic Mind could not stand in front of, or walk around, a house.) But yet the house is not a thing in itself but only an appearance. So "What, then, am I to understand by the question: how the manifold may be connected in the appearance itself, which yet is nothing in itself?"

Kant then says that we must "unfold the transcendental meaning" of our concept of an object. Kant's only explicit definition of "transcendental" is given in the Introduction at A12, where Kant says, "I entitle transcendental all knowledge which is occupied not so much with objects as with the mode of our knowledge of objects, in so far as this mode of knowledge is to be possible a priori." So unfolding the transcendental meaning of this concept can only mean asking ourselves what exactly we *mean* by "object of awareness," especially in view of the fact that we have a priori knowledge of how this external referent of consciousness must be. When I do this, Kant says, I realize that "the house is not a thing in itself, but only a representation, the transcendental object of which is unknown." In this passage "transcendental object" must mean thing in itself; it must be that object which, a few lines earlier, Kant has said "affects" us to produce representations, but which is itself "entirely outside our sphere of knowledge." Here Kant's correspondence theory of consciousness is in evidence. This sort of object, however, is not what Kant is concerned with here. His interest in the second Analogy is with the "object" of a coherence theory of knowledge, that object which is thought into experience by the mind. This coherence theory object is the spatio-temporal world of appearance which is in some sense distinct from representations and in some sense not.

Kant finally tells us how it can be that "the appearance which is given to me, notwithstanding the fact that it is nothing but the sum of these representations, is viewed as their object." This appearance can be "represented," thought of, as an object distinct from those states of myself of which I am immediately conscious "only if it [appearance] stands under a rule which distinguishes it from every other apprehension and necessitates some one particular mode of connection of the manifold." Kant then says that "the *object* is that in the appearance which contains the condition of this necessary rule of apprehension."

This is clearly Kant's coherence theory of the relation of consciousness to its object. The only way in which I can distinguish a succession of representations which is an awareness of a real world from a succession which is only a series of states of myself (since "we have to deal only with our representations") is through the fact that the former succession is necessary in some sense. The object of awareness is viewed here just as Kant portrays it in the Transcendental Deduction. He sees this object as the source of the necessity in the order of my representations, as "that in the appearance"—here the internal flow of representations in the subject—"which contains the condition of this *necessary* rule of apprehension," i.e., which forces my states of mind to occur in a particular way. Because necessity, and hence a priori knowability, is in Kant's view imposed by the mind rather than being given from without, the implication of this paragraph is that the appearance as *object* of representations (that is, the physical world of things in space and time) is just the *necessity* which the mind thinks into its own subjective states. I do distinguish between my representations and the physical world which some of them are "of," and I do this not, as Hume suggests, through the degree of vividness of the sensory data but rather by means of the necessity in their ordering. I say that the order of my sensory data is necessitated by "how things really are" in the space-time world which I am perceiving. But for Kant this physical world is a logical construct in the sense that the only hard facts there are, are facts about the representations of "the subject" and their internally imposed order. Only in this manner can I *distinguish between* the order of my representations and the order of things in the world and at the same time *infer from* one to the other.

The remainder of the second Analogy bears out this interpretation. At A192 Kant asks what difference it makes within the consciousness of the subject whether the subject is witnessing an event or is surveying an unchanging object. The only difference, he says, is that in the former case there is a necessity in the sequence of representations. In watching a ship move downstream, we say that the order of things out in the world makes our representations occur in a certain sequence, whereas when we are surveying a house we can (within limits) have our representations in any order. To explain, then, what it means to witness a real event out in the world, since "we have only to deal with our representations," we must "derive the *subjective succession* of apprehension from the *objective succession* of appearances." That is, we must explain how the necessity or non-necessity of my order of representations is related to facts about appearances. The subjective succession, however, purely *qua* subjective succession, is "altogether arbitrary." In my sensory data themselves there is nothing which necessitates any particular order of their occurrence. But since an order of things which was altogether distinct from these representations would be a thing in itself and hence "nothing to me," this real, objective succession of appearances "will therefore consist in that order of the manifold of appearance [the order of representations in the mind] according to which, in conformity with a rule, the apprehension of that which happens follows upon the apprehension of that which precedes." In other words, to say that an objective succession occurs out in the world "is only another way of saying that I cannot arrange the apprehension other than in this very succession."

Having thus reduced the real sequence of states in the world to the necessity of the order of states of mind in the subject, Kant then employs several arguments—the exact number is a matter of debate among Kant scholars—which attempt to push this necessity of subjective sequence back into the world of appearance. His aim, of course, is to reach the conclusion that it is a necessary condition of experience that successive states of the world be related as cause and effect. However dubious we may be about the validity of these arguments, we can see that Strawson is not quite right in attributing "a non-sequitur of numbing grossness" to Kant here.[24] Strawson attributes to Kant the following bad argument: I witness a real sequence of states A-B out in the world. Therefore, the sequence of representations in my mind will necessarily have the order a-b. Therefore, the original sequence in the world must *also* necessarily have the order A-B, which is to say that state A must *cause* state B. Strawson argues that the only sort of causal relation which is required for our being able to infer an A-B sequence in the world from an a-b sequence in the mind is one between a real state in the world and the representation in the mind which it produces, rather than one between states A and B themselves.

If Kant were "regarding appearances as things in themselves," then he would indeed be guilty of the mistake which Strawson attributes to him. If objects in the physical world were ontologically distinct from representations in the mind, then one could not argue from necessity in the mind to any necessity out in the world. It is only if states A-B in the world are *in some sense* nothing over and above representations a-b as states of the subject that necessity in the a-b sequence can imply anything about necessity between A and B. And this is, in fact, the case in Kant's picture of things. Yet Kant's argument still, I am afraid, will not work. If the real sequence A-B is just the necessity of the subjective sequence a-b, then it will still be a mistake simply from this subjective necessity to infer causal necessity (or any other kind of necessity) in the "real" sequence A-B. Kant is led into this mistake, I believe, largely through the ambiguity of the term, "appearance." In A195, for example, Kant says that, "I render my subjective synthesis of apprehension objective only by reference to a rule in accordance with which the appearances in their succession, that is, as they happen, are determined by the preceding state."

---

[24]Strawson, *Bounds of Sense*, 137-38.

Here "appearance" means the subjective sequence of mental states a-b, which are "rendered objective" by the necessity in their temporal order. However, "appearance" is also used by Kant to designate the objective sequence A-B, which is a logical construct out of a-b. So it is only through the ambiguity of "appearance" that Kant is able to infer from the necessity in the sequence of conscious states to the (causal) necessity of states in the space-time world.

Another portion of the second Analogy which should be mentioned as an illustration of Kant's "necessary connection" view of the outward reference of consciousness is the paragraph at A197. This is also a quite clear example of Kant's Cartesian starting point *contra* Strawson. Kant begins by saying that we can become conscious of "representations in us," which he describes as "inner determinations of our mind in this or that relation of time." He then asks a version of Descartes's question: "How, then, does it come about that we posit an object from these representations, and so, in addition to their subjective reality, as modifications, ascribe to them some mysterious kind of objective reality?" This "objective" status of a representation, as being "of" a real world, cannot consist merely in its *de facto* association with another representation, for the same question could then be asked about this second representation, the question of what makes it "of an object." Kant concludes that

> if we enquire what new character *relation to an object* confers upon our representations, what dignity they thereby acquire, we find that it results only in subjecting the representations to a rule, and so in necessitating us to connect them in some one specific manner; and conversely, that only in so far as our representations are necessitated in a certain order as regards their time-relations do they acquire objective meaning.

In this talk about states of mind and their relation to the space-time world which some of them are "of," there is no doubt about what is being reduced to what. For Kant, the ultimately existing things are "inner determinations of our mind." Kant is careful here to avoid the question of whose mind is "ours," so that we cannot be sure if his starting point is Cartesian in the sense of viewing each person as trapped inside his own *individual* consciousness. His starting point (and finishing point) is definitely idealist, however, in the sense that what is really real are mental entities and processes. The objective, physical world is reduced to the necessity in the ordering of these mental components.

Through the remainder of the second Analogy, Kant repeats this general theme and uses various arguments which attempt to push the necessity of the order of representations out into the physical world where it can become the causal connection between states of the world. He is quite explicit that it is the understanding, a faculty "in us," which injects the necessary order into representations and hence is responsible for causal connection in the phenomenal world. At A201 Kant again speaks of the difference between merely having representations in one's consciousness and being conscious of an object. He says,

> If this synthesis [of representations in a single consciousness] is a synthesis of apprehension of the manifold of a given appearance, the order is determined in the object, or to speak more correctly, is an order of successive synthesis that determines an object.

This is as clear a confirmation as there could be that for Kant it is not the order of states out in the world ("in the object") which determines the order of representations; rather, it is just the opposite—the necessary order of representations in the mind is what "determines an object," is what *makes* the representations an awareness of a real world.

Kant's Use of "Real" in the Text

My claim is that Kant's concept of the transcendental object, in those passages in the *Critique* where this does not refer to the thing in itself, can be described as our concept of simply the object of our awareness and knowledge as such, prior to any further description of this object. We would also describe this as our concept of "how things really are" or "the real world" or "objective reality per se." In making this claim about the proper interpretation of Kant's philosophy, however, I should relate it to Kant's own use of such expressions as "real" and "objectively real." Unfortunately, Kant is no more consistent in his use of these terms than he is with most of his philosophical vocabulary. His inconsistent use of "real" is partly the result of the unresolved conflict in his philosophy between his correspondence and his coherence views of consciousness.

The majority of uses of "real" and related expressions in the *Critique* are in connection with Kant's coherence view of the relation of consciousness to its object. In this context Kant generally applies the term "objective reality" to concepts, saying that the objective reality (or objective validity) of a concept is, or depends upon, its application to some intuition (A235, A239, B413). Using just the term "reality," Kant tells us that "reality, in the pure concept of the understanding, is that which corresponds to sensation in general" (A143). In this particular passage Kant is attempting to establish reality as one of the categories of the understanding alongside substance, causation, and all the rest. What he says about this "category," however, shows that this attempt must represent Kant's architectonic at work. The concept of the transcendental object, i.e., the mind's overall capacity for synthesis, is our concept of objective reality itself. The individual categories, in turn, are included within this wider concept; they tell us more precisely what "objectively real" *means* to the human mind. Kant, however, tells us that the concept of the transcendental object and the categories which it comprises *have* reality, which is to say that there is in fact "given" to the mind sensory data to which these concepts apply. The mind's overall capacity for conceptualization or synthesis, according to Kant, provides for the intentionality of consciousness; it is what enables consciousness to reach out to a real world. Because our understanding cannot produce its own sensory data, however, a further prerequisite for human knowledge is that there exist "given" data which are presented to the understanding through the sensibility. Therefore as Kant (usually) uses the term "reality," reality is not itself a category but is rather a fact about the categories and about all other valid concepts, the fact of their applicability to the data with which we are presented in experience.

I believe that our own use of "real" can be related fairly easily to Kant's employment of this term. We do not generally speak of concepts either as being real or as having objective reality; we rather attribute this quality to the objects of our concepts so as to say, for example, that elephants are real and unicorns are not. But we could express this same point in not overly technical language by saying that our concept of an elephant, unlike our concept of a unicorn, applies to something. And if we ask what "applying to something" means, from within our experience, we might reply in Kantian language that in the course of our experience we are presented with sensory data, or intuitions, which are properly handled by our concept of an elephant, and that this never happens with the concept which we have of a unicorn. This example leaves it quite undecided what a concept is or what it means to apply a concept to sensory data, and so it does not commit us to anything like Kant's coherence theory of consciousness. My point is only that it would not require a very drastic change in our normal ways of speaking to say with Kant that certain *concepts* are real and others are not and that the reality of a concept depends upon its connection with what we are presented with in experience.

Speaking in this way we would say that the reality of what Kant calls an empirical concept cannot be known *a priori*. We must wait to see which sensory data present themselves in order to see which of our concepts apply to these data and which do not. Our pure concepts, though, and the single concept of which these are determinations, are guaranteed to have objective reality. These will necessarily apply to any sensory data which are capable of being combined in a single experience. We cannot, however, read this off from these concepts themselves. Thus there is no *logical* necessity that everything should have a cause or that changing entities should be manifestations of an underlying, permanent substance. Propositions asserting these truths are not analytic but synthetic. Their a priori status can be shown only by a transcendental argument which establishes that the application of these concepts is a necessary condition of experience. What Kant aims to show is simply that *if* we are to have experience at all, it must be *of* a world of substances in causal relation. The same is true for that largest of all concepts, our concept of the transcendental object (or, in my contention, "real world"). There is no guarantee from within this concept that there is anything to which the concept applies. That is, it is not logically necessary that there should exist any real world at all. Again, all that Kant can aim to show is that if we have experience, which requires a unity of sensory data in one consciousness, this experience must be *of* a real world which has those features specified by the categories.

This argument is, Kant believes, enough to answer Descartes's question in the *Meditations*. Descartes would admit that he possesses in his mind the concept of "real world" or "object of my consciousness." He must have this concept in order to ask the questions which he asks. His concern is that this concept may not apply to anything, that there may not in fact *be* any real world at all. Kant's attempt at a transcendental deduction of the categories can be seen as a response to Descartes's concern. Kant does not actually "deduce" any of the particular categories in that part of the first *Critique* which he calls his Transcendental Deduction. What we find here is rather a deduction, or justification, of that largest concept of which the individual categories are determinations, the concept of the "object in general" or real world per se. Kant gives a transcendental justification of this concept by attempting to show that one cannot have consciousness at all without this consciousness having precisely that status of being "of an object" which Descartes fears that it may lack. Kant attempts to show, therefore, that our concept *of* objective reality must *have* objective reality in the Kantian sense.

This use of "real" is connected with Kant's coherence theory of the relation of consciousness to its object. In this view the space-time world is indeed real because certain necessary features of it constitute what "real" *means*; but the very realness of this world is thought into it by the knowing subject. Yet Kant also has another use of "real"—one which does not square with this use at all—in a connection with his correspondence theory of consciousness. According to this view it is the thing in itself which is truly, ultimately real. The phenomenal world, by contrast is (only) appearance. Examples of this usage are not difficult to find in the first *Critique*. Thus Kant says that the thing in itself is "indeed real per se," but is unknown to us (Bxx), that time does not possess "absolute reality" (A35), and that the very concept of appearance "establishes the objective reality of noumena" (A249). All of this fits poorly with Kant's other uses of "real"; it shows simply that Kant means different things by "real" depending on which view of consciousness he is espousing in a particular passage.

A recent writer, Jonathan Bennett, recognizes this ambiguity in Kant's use of "real."[25] Unlike other commentators on Kant (see above, 53-54), Bennett insists that Kant's "basic position" (i.e., his coherence view of consciousness) restricts the concept of reality to the space-time world. He admits, however, that Kant sometimes falls into a "betrayal" of this legitimate use of "real" when he speaks of the thing in itself, in contrast to the phenomenal world, as what is "real in itself." This lapse from what Bennett calls Kant's concept-empiricism is, of course, required by Kant's correspondence theory of consciousness with its attendent doctrine of the thing in itself and is also needed for Kant's moral theory.

The Relation of Kant's Two Theories of Consciousness in the Text

For the most part Kant keeps his two different theories of consciousness, and hence his two different accounts of "real," separate in the first *Critique*. The correspondence theory, while not explicitly argued for

---

[25]Jonathan Bennett, *Kant's Dialectic* (London: Cambridge University Press, 1974) 49-53.

anywhere, appears most prominently in the Transcendental Aesthetic. This is no doubt because the correspondence view is connected primarily with Kant's notion of sensibility, especially his idea that this is a passive faculty to which something must be "given" from without. The coherence view, by contrast, is developed in those parts of the *Critique* which are concerned with the operation of the understanding, namely the Transcendental Deduction and parts of the Second Analogy. In these parts of the text, it should be noted, there is almost no mention of the thing in itself. The passage which I have found most clearly to combine, or try to combine, both views in a single statement is in the Transcendental Dialectic in the sixth section of the Antinomy of Pure Reason. In the portion of the text beginning at A493, Kant says that the objects of experience "have no existence" outside of our experience, and he then defines as real whatever "stands in connection with a perception in accordance with the laws of empirical advance." This statement is in line with his coherence view, according to which our concept of "objectively real" is just the mind's capacity for synthesis as such. But Kant then immediately alludes to another sort of reality when he says that these objects of experience are not "real in themselves, that is, outside this advance of experience."

Kant says more about objects and reality in A494 where, speaking of the receptive nature of the sensibility, he says that representations in the mind, to the extent that they are properly "connected" and are "determinable according to laws of the unity of experience," constitute the objects of our experience. But then Kant thinks of another kind of object:

> The nonsensible cause of these representations is completely unknown to us, and cannot therefore be intuited by us as object . . . We may, however, entitle the purely intelligible cause of appearances in general the transcendental object, but merely in order to have something corresponding to sensibility viewed as a receptivity.

In this paragraph we see both of Kant's views of the relation of consciousness to its object. There is one kind of "object" which is a function of the connection of representations in a single consciousness—this is the object which is thought into experience by the activities of the understanding. But then there is a second kind of object, namely the transcendental object. Here this must be the thing in itself as the cause of representations. It is in this passage that Kant seems to see most clearly that there are two quite different "objects of experience" which he is dealing with, but Kant does not ask himself whether he truly needs both of them.

In the sentences immediately following we have chaos:

> To this transcendental object we can ascribe the whole extent and connection of our possible perceptions, and can say that it is given in itself prior to all experience. But the appearances, while conforming to it, are not given in themselves, but only in this experience, being mere representations, which as perceptions can mark out a real object only in so far as the perception connects with all others according to the rules of the unity of experience. Thus we can say that the real things of past time are given in the transcendental object of experience.

In this first sentence the transcendental object must again be the reference to an external reality which is thought into experience according to the coherence theory, for the thing in itself is surely not responsible for the *connection* of our perceptions. But then to say that this is "given," and given prior to experience, sounds like a blatant contradiction. "Prior to experience" indicates that we are dealing with the concept of unity (= reality) per se, which connects what is given *in experience* into a single consciousness. On the other hand, it is only if the transcendental object is the "object" in the correspondence view that it could be in any sense "given"; but then of course it would *not* be "prior to experience." In the second sentence above, if appearances "conform to" the transcendental object, then this must, again, be the "object" of Kant's coherence theory, which is responsible for enabling perceptions to "mark out" a real thing through their internal connection. And finally, what it can mean, in the final sentence, for anything to be "given in the transcendental object of experience" is beyond my surmise. This entire passage is of interest because it is the most striking instance in the entire first *Critique* and the *Prolegomena* of Kant's two theories of the object of consciousness appearing together, locked in mortal combat.

The Refutation of Idealism

There is one final portion of the first *Critique* which needs to be examined in connection with the question of what sort of idealism Kant espouses. This is the well-known and much analyzed Refutation of Idealism, which appears only in the second edition of the *Critique*. Actually, there are three areas of text which need to be considered here: the first Analogy of Experience, which the Refutation of Idealism pretty clearly rests upon; the Refutation itself; and a long footnote to the Refutation which, for some reason, Kant inserts into the Preface of the second edition of the *Critique*. The argument in these sections is often thought to be incompatible with other parts of the first *Critique*, especially the fourth Paralogism in the first edition. (See above, 37-40.) Kant appears to be responding in the Refutation to the Cartesian notion of imprisonment in one's individual consciousness and its corollary doubt about the existence of an external world; and he seems here to be arguing for a solution to this problem which is quite different from, and less idealist than, that which is presented in the fourth Paralogism.

There is considerable repetition in Kant's statement of his first Analogy, but the argument may be summarized as follows: There is something called the unity of consciousness, which involves a number of different states of mind being tied together in a single experience. Because time is the form of inner sense, this single experience must include successive representations occurring in a single duration of time; the unity of apperception, which involves the subject's awareness that "all of *my* representations are *mine*," will therefore include also an awareness of this one time in which all of the subject's representations occur. But Kant tells us that "time itself cannot be perceived" and infers from this that there must exist in the object of our experience (the phenomenal world) "the substratum which represents time in general." The substratum is substance, the underlying stuff, the total quantity of which can be neither increased nor decreased and of which all particular physical objects are modifications. This permanent substance is what "represents" the unity of time, and it is therefore a condition of my awareness of anything as being in a single time. And because time is the form of inner sense and is hence the sensible mode under which we apprehend anything whatever, this awareness of permanent substance in the space-time world is a necessary condition of experience.

I must confess that I have never been able to see the validity of this argument, and I have gotten little help from the secondary literature. What eludes me is the force of the "therefore" which Kant inserts between "I am aware of things as being in a single time, but time is not itself perceived," and "there must be a permanent substratum as a part or aspect of what I perceive." It seems to me that some additional steps are required here, but I cannot ascertain what these connecting steps might be.²⁶ But let us suppose that Kant's argument is valid and that the object of our experience must indeed contain the permanent substratum. Will such an admission have any weighty implications regarding the reality of the physical world? I believe that it will not. Because of Kant's Copernican Revolution, Kant must say that this permanent substance which necessarily characterizes the phenomenal world is itself thought into this world by the understanding. And now, whether there is literally *one* phenomenal world, and *one* time, and *one* underlying substratum will depend upon the relation between the thinking subject and individual human persons. Kant comes no closer to addressing this question in the Analogy than he does anywhere else in the *Critique,* and so for this reason this Analogy, even if it presented a valid argument, would not tell us much about the kind of reality which Kant attributes to the space-time world.

The Refutation of Idealism is directed against the "problematic" idealism which Descartes maintains at the beginning of his *Meditations.* Unfortunately, Kant does not give us much of an account of the Cartesian view, which makes it difficult to know exactly what he is attempting to refute. He says only that this kind of idealism "pleads incapacity to prove, through immediate experience, any existence except our own" (B275). To refute such a view, Kant says, we must establish "that we have *experience,* and not merely imagination of outer things" and that our "inner experience," which Descartes accepts as beyond question, "is possible only on the assumption of outer experience." Next Kant gives the formal "Thesis" of his Refutation, which is that "the mere, but empirically determined, consciousness of my own existence proves the existence of objects in space outside me." A person who had read only Descartes's *Meditations* plus these opening sentences of Kant's Refutation would naturally think that Kant was trying to prove that the individual subject of experience, through his awareness of his own states of mind, can be sure that there exists a spatial realm of material things which he is aware of in normal perception and which exists *as* a spatial realm quite independently of this subject as *individual* knower. This is,

---

²⁶A good account of the unclarity of Kant's intentions and arguments in the Refutation, and of the different interpretations which have resulted from the unclarity, is contained in Paul Guyer's book, *Kant and the Claims of Knowledge* (New York: Cambridge University Press, 1987) 280-84.

after all, what Descartes thinks he has proven by the end of the *Meditations* to satisfy his own initial doubt. But with the complexity which we have seen in Kant's conception of the subject of experience and in his view of the relation of consciousness to its object, we should look very carefully at just what Kant proves, and intends to prove, under the description "objects in space outside me."

Kant begins the Refutation by stating the conclusion of the first Analogy: "All determination of time presupposes something permanent in perception." In my awareness of myself, therefore, which involves an awareness of all of my representations as being within a single duration of time, I must be aware of something which is absolutely permanent. But this permanent thing "cannot be something in me." Why it cannot is not made clear (to me) in Kant's arguments either in the Refutation itself or in the footnote to it in the second edition Preface. Why could not the understanding which thinks permanence—underlying substance—into outer sense think it into inner sense as well? If such were the case, I would be aware of my representations as modifications of a persisting ego. This permanent ego would, of course, characterize me only as I appear to myself and not as I am in my own nature, but it would nevertheless be as phenomenally real as physical matter.

Kant does seem to address himself briefly to this question in the Refutation, where at B278 he tells us (as he will repeat often in the Paralogisms) that the "I think" of apperception contains no intuition and therefore nothing which "as permanent, might serve as correlate for the determination of time in inner sense." Somewhat later in the *Critique* Kant says that an intuition of space is required for the application of our pure concept of substance, "For space alone is determined as permanent, while time, and therefore everything that is in inner sense, is in constant flux" (B291). I must confess that these very brief arguments are not clear to me, and I suspect that for them to become clear one would have to understand Kant's doctrine of inner sense, which is by all accounts one of the more difficult parts of the Kantian philosophy. So let us accept for the sake of argument that there is in fact nothing permanent in my awareness of myself in inner sense. Where does the argument go from here?

It goes immediately to Kant's conclusion that "perception of this permanent is possible only through a *thing* outside me, and not through the mere *representation* of a thing outside me," and thus that my awareness of myself in inner sense "is possible only through the existence of actual things which I perceive outside me." In assessing this argument, the first thing to note is its dependence on the conclusion of the first Analogy—that awareness of time demands an awareness of something permanent. The Refutation of Idealism can be no stronger than this premise on which it rests. If we accept this premise and also admit that there is no awareness of anything permanent in inner sense, then (if inner sense and outer sense exhaust the possible forms of consciousness) we must accept Kant's conclusion that we are aware of something permanent in outer sense. But as Kant admits, there is no permanent sensory datum in any sort of consciousness. The permanent is rather something which the understanding thinks into its sensory data when it combines these data into a single consciousness and thus refers its consciousness outward as an awareness of a real world. This is why Kant is so insistent that outer sense, which necessarily contains an awareness of the permanent, must be a *real awareness* of "something outside of me." It cannot be only a stream of inner consciousness with no relation to an object, as Descartes fears it might be.

At this point we must remember that according to Kant's coherence theory of consciousness, the difference between a series of intuitions or sensory data which are mere states of the subject and a series of intuitions which constitute a real awareness of an external reality is that in the case of "real awareness" these intuitions have been synthesized into a single consciousness by the activity of the understanding. And one necessary aspect of this activity is the category of substance, which results in the "object" of this unified consciousness being a material world in which all things are modifications of an underlying, permanent substratum. Thus Kant's Refutation of Idealism, with its insistence on a "real awareness" of an external world, and his view that the permanence of substance will accompany, or result from, this "real awareness," rests on his coherence theory of the outward reference of consciousness. Thus, in turn, should make us properly dubious about Kant's claims to have reassured the Cartesian against his doubt about the external world.

Again, everything will depend here upon our question of who is the Kantian subject. If it is the individual person, then Kant's Refutation, if taken in the context of the coherence theory upon which it rests, will not answer Descartes but rather confirm him in his solipsistic nightmares.[27]

---

[27]Robert Paul Wolff would disagree with this. See below, 96-98.

But if the subject is not the individual person and if by means of a cosmic Mind or some other such thing Kant succeeds in giving us a single space and time in which all of us individual subjects exist, this situation will then leave the individual Cartesian in the same state of doubt in which he started: How can he *as an individual mind* be sure that there is a public world in which he exists and of which his individual consciousness gives him knowledge?

For all of these reasons, I do not think that Kant's Refutation of Idealism is worthy of the excitement which it has caused among commentators on the first *Critique*. The Refutation shows us that Kant was unhappy with the form of idealism which was attributed to him upon publication of the first edition of the *Critique* and that he wanted to put some philosophical distance between himself and certain other thinkers. It does not, I think, tell us much more than this. First of all, the argument does not work since it rests upon the first Analogy. Secondly, even if the argument did succeed in proving what Kant wants it to prove, Kant's reasoning here would be of little help to the reader in understanding what form of idealism Kant espouses in the first *Critique* or how he differs from philosophers such as Berkeley and Descartes. The question of what, Kant intends to prove by this argument is tied up with the other questions about the status of the subject of experience and the relation of consciousness to its object on which Kant speaks with more than one voice in the *Critique*. Until these latter questions are settled, the argument is of little value to us in our attempts to understand what sort of reality Kant attributes to the physical world and what sort of idealism he takes himself to have refuted.

Chapter 4

Summary.
Possible Interpretations
of Kant's Idealism

In surveying the massive amount of literature on Kant, one is struck by how difficult it must be at this date to say anything truly new about Kant's philosophy. Kant's difficulties with the identity of the knowing subject are discussed at length by Strawson and are also given attention in the commentaries by Wolff and Paton. Kant's two different views about the outward reference of consciousness are noted by Paton (who describes the conflict between these two theories as "a difficulty of the Critical Philosophy as a whole")[1] and are stated succinctly by Henry E. Allison in "Kant's Concept of the Transcendental Object."[2] And of course the controversies about the thing in itself and about Kant's transcendental idealism stretch back to Kant's own lifetime. It is impossible for any writer to have covered more than a small portion of the literature on Kant's philosophy[3] and it is therefore risky for a commentator to claim absolute originality in his interpretation. It is enough, perhaps, in this present work if I may strive for clarity in showing that there truly are conflicting directions in Kant's thought regarding the identity of the form-imposing subject and its relation to its object, and in showing how

---

[1] Paton, *Kant's Metaphysics*, 2:425.
[2] Henry E. Allison, "Kant's Concept of the Transcendental Object," *Kant-Studien* 68 (1959): 166-86.
[3] Guenter Zoeller tells us that "Over the past twenty-five years, scholarship on Kant has taken on colossal proportions, affectively defying summary assessment and manageable presentation." See Zoeller, "Main Developments in Recent Scholarship on the *Critique of Pure Reason*" in *Philosophy and Phenomenological Research* 53 (1993): 445.

these two unresolved parts of Kant's system bear upon one another with implications regarding solipsism and the public objectivity of the physical world. Given these opposing tendencies, the following doctrines might be attributed to Kant.

If we adopt Kant's correspondence view of "of an object" and interpret the subject of experience as the individual person, we will have something like Paton's interpretation of Kant. There will be a sort of public world in the sense that there really is something, namely "the object," which each of us apprehends in the same way *as* a physical universe due to each person's own necessary, mind-imposed conditions of experience. Whether this object is taken to be "that which appears" or rather as the cause of appearances (= representations) in the mind, there will not be literally one phenomenal world or one space and time. There will rather be "the object" (with its own inherent nature) which appears as a single phenomenal world to the individual subject; and there will be as many separate instances of this "appearing as a single world" as there are subjects of experience.

If we take Kant's coherence view of consciousness and regard the Kantian subject as the individual person, problems of solipsism will be insurmountable. For if we say that the reference of my consciousness to a real world is no more than its unity in a single experience, the person who is plagued by Cartesian doubt will hardly feel reassured. He will feel that we have confirmed him in his worst fears that he and his consciousness may be all that exist and then given him a Pickwickean "solution" to his problem by choosing to call a certain purely internal aspect of his consciousness its relation to a real world. The Cartesian would be particularly puzzled about how a person who adopted such a view could maintain a belief in other minds. For if the phenomenal world, all that I can mean by "objective reality," is only a function of *my* consciousness, what sense could I possibly make of the idea of *another* consciousness?

In connection with these difficulties it is interesting to consider Robert Paul Wolff's defense of Kant in his commentary. Wolff, unlike Strawson, takes very seriously Kant's "imaginary subject of transcendental psychology" as manifested in the doctrine of synthesis. Therefore Wolff, also unlike Strawson, puts great emphasis on Kant's "necessary connection" theory of the relation of consciousness to its object, and he regards this as Kant's considered view. But Wolff also takes the Kantian subject of experience to be the individual person, primarily because of the difficulties which he sees in viewing the subject as anything else.

Summary. Possible Interpretations of Kant's Idealism

With this combination of doctrines and with his determination to defend Kant's theory of knowledge, as so interpreted, as the truth about consciousness, Wolff is faced with the task of answering the disappointed Cartesian. This he does in a remarkable discussion at the very end of his commentary.[4] He says that Kant's answer to the sceptic, or the Cartesian who fears that his consciousness may have no object at all, begins by substituting for "object" the notion of "concept of an object." That is, rather than asking, "How do I know that my consciousness is *of* a real world?" Kant asks, "How does my concept of 'object of my experience' function within my experience; what difference does the use of this concept make to me?" In answer to this question, of course, Kant develops the doctrine that the relation of my consciousness to an "object" or real world is nothing more than its unity as one experience. Wolff sees that the Cartesian may find this maneuver unsatisfying and that this "epistemological turn" might seem to be "only a sophisticated surrender to the most extreme forms of scepticism." As Wolff says, "Universality and necessity may indeed be among the marks of knowledge, but there is also the belief in an object 'out there,' standing over against the subject. If that has been lost, then the result is scepticism, no matter what one calls it."

Continuing this battle with his imaginary opponent, Wolff replies, "This criticism is extremely hard to meet, though I believe it to be totally without force." He urges that Kant's system can allow that physical objects are real, in at least most of our ordinary sense of this term. But does not our ordinary sense of "real" include the idea of, as Wolff says, "an ontologically independent object?" To this Wolff replies that if it does, it ought not to: "Universality and necessity are all you can get, Kant says in effect. Therefore, they are all it has ever been legitimate to demand." But suppose a person persists in believing, or wanting to believe, that the space-time world in which he lives is something which exists independent of himself as an individual knowing subject, and that furthermore he can come to know something about how this world is "in itself," in that nature of its own which it has and which it would have had even if this particular knowing person had not existed at all. Such a person, Wolff says, must "simply be dismissed as unserious," and he

---

[4]Wolff, *Kant's Theory*, 319-24.

adds that, "In the terminology of a later school, he needs to be cured, not answered."

This passage shows how far a commentator can be moved to go in defending Kant. Wolff says that we must reject the very idea of an "ontologically independent object" of our consciousness or knowledge. This raises the question: Independent of what, exactly? Wolff soft-pedals his position slightly here, as do so many defenders as Kant, by saying that we cannot know anything about an object "independently of the conditions of its being known." In a sense, of course, this is trivially true. If there are certain features of an object which I must think about if I am to succeed in thinking about anything at all, then certainly I cannot conceive of any object independently of *these* features. But Kant's view is much stronger than this. His doctrine, especially in the coherence view of consciousness which Wolff adopts, is that all of these necessary features, including the very existence of the object of awareness as a real object at all, are a function of the synthetic activities of the understanding. Furthermore, in the interpretation which Wolff adopts, against the interpretations of Kemp-Smith and Schrader, the understanding which does all of this is a faculty of the individual person.

Such a philosophical position, for the person who held it, would seem to make the world a lonely place. If the world which I am aware of is literally a creation of my individual mental activities, then what about the other persons who inhabit this world? Are they also products of the synthesis of my representations into a single consciousness? Or does each of them have his own private objective reality which he constructs out of his own sensory data? Either way, communication between us would seem to be a problem, as would, indeed, even being able to conceive of another mind as a subject of consciousness different from oneself. All of this shows, I believe, that to the extent that one accepts Kant's "necessary connection" view of consciousness and its relation to its object, one will be pushed toward positing a world soul or "one universal consciousness" as the creative subject of experience. As I have noted above, there is some indication in the text of the *Critique* that Kant himself was aware of these pressures.

It should be added here that there is one other possible combination of doctrines in Kant. One could accept the correspondence view of the relation of consciousness to its object and at the same time regard the subject who imposes space, time, and the categories as something "larger than" individual persons. One would than have the thing in itself, which

Summary. Possible Interpretations of Kant's Idealism

would be the intrinsic nature of that "object" which appears to the Subject as a space-time world, and all of us individual persons would then be part of this object-as-it-appears. I cannot see that there is much to be said for this view either as an interpretation of Kant or as a theory to be taken seriously in its own right. It is hard for me to make comprehensible, let alone persuasive, the notion that I am part of the way something which is unknown to me appears to another thing which is unknown to me. As an interpretation of the development of Kant's thought, it is more plausible to suppose that Kant began with the correspondence theory of consciousness and the subject as individual person and that he then developed the coherence view of consciousness. In working out this coherence view, however, he also continued to adhere to the correspondence theory and to the doctrine of the thing in itself which is an implication of it. (The fact that some version of this doctrine is required for Kant's moral theory may have contributed to Kant's retention of the correspondence view of consciousness.) And in working out his coherence view Kant was at the same time pushed toward a conception of the subject of experience as "one universal consciousness" to allow for a single phenomenal world.

So did Kant believe that the space-time world is real in the sense in which we believe that it is real? Part of our common sense view, surely is that the reality of this world involves at least its independence of us as individual human beings. This is how I distinguish an animal in my dreams or hallucinations, which I call unreal because its existence depends upon its literally being part of my individual consciousness, from the elephant which I see in a zoo, which is real in the sense of existing and being what it is quite independent of me and of my thoughts about it. Did Kant believe that the space-time world is real in this sense of being independent of the particular human perceivers and thinkers who occupy it? To this question we can only say that under some interpretations of his doctrines the world is real in this sense and under other interpretations of them it is not. If we ask which of these interpretations Kant himself finally settled on, our answer can only be that he did not settle on any of them. This is one reason why Kant's philosophy is so difficult to understand. The one thing which we may conclude is that the label of "empirically real and transcendentally ideal" does not express a single doctrine about the status of the physical world, just as "transcendental idealism" fails to denote a single kind of idealism.

Chapter 5

The Sources of Kant's Different Idealist Doctrines

Much of what I have said in chapters 2 and 3 points to the source of the conflicting idealistic doctrines in Kant's philosophy, in the conflicting demands of his theories of perception and thought. In this much shorter chapter I shall be content mainly to summarize these considerations.

If one had to specify the single most important insight in the Kantian philosophy, surely Kant's distinction between perception and thought would be a good candidate for this status. The distinction itself was certainly a common one prior to Kant, and goes back at least as far as Plato. Philosophers before Kant, however, tended to emphasize one of these at the expense of the other and to regard one of them as a confused or faded or otherwise debased form of the other. Much of the battle in Kant's day between (and among) the Continental philosophers and the British philosophers had to do with which of these, perception or thought, represented the valuable, dominant end of the continuum of "ideas" upon which they were supposedly both located. Kant was the first to see clearly that perception and thought are not on a continuum at all but are intrinsically different mental activities. Kant also saw that each of these is crucial to the attainment of knowledge, that no awareness *of* anything *as* anything could be had by dispensing with one or the other of these components of experience. If Kant had done nothing else, this single philosophical move would be enough to assure his place in the history of Western thought.

Unfortunately for Kant's own philosophy, however, Kant not only makes this distinction but also adopts different forms of idealism in connection with each of the components of experience. These two kinds of idealism do not fit together, and this fact prevents Kant's doctrines of the sensibility and the understanding from meshing smoothly. Kant attempts to express the interaction of sensibility and understanding in his assertion that "through the sensibility objects are *given*, through the understanding objects are *thought*." But the sort of mind that can utilize the faculty of sensibility (as Kant conceives this faculty) and the kind that can use the faculty of understanding (as Kant conceives it) are quite different. Likewise, the sort of object that can be "given" and the sort that can be "thought" are quite different.

It is not altogether surprising that Kant's theories of perception and thought do not fit together. Without accepting all of the details of the "patchwork" theory of the composition of the *Critique of Pure Reason*, as developed by Vaihinger and others, it is at least obvious that Kant's views of perception and thought were developed at different times. Kant's doctrine of sensibility was developed at least as early as his *Inaugural Dissertation* of 1769. This is the first work in which Kant declares space and time to be "subjective" forms of intuition which characterize the objects of perceptual awareness only as they appear. At this stage in the development of his doctrines, Kant still clung to the hope that the intellect could penetrate the veil of sense and attain knowledge of things in themselves. In the *Inaugural Dissertation* there is every reason to think that the "intuition" which is the source of space and time is just the perceptual apparatus and perceptual activities of the individual human mind. And there is no reason why Kant should not make this identification: If space and time are mind-imposed, but existence, unity, plurality, etc., characterize objects (and subjects) of experience in themselves, then there could perfectly well exist a plurality of minds plus independent objects acting causally to "affect" these minds.

There is a passage in the *Prolegomena* that seems to express something like the perceptual phenomenalism and intellectual rationalism of the *Inaugural Dissertation*. In this passage Kant denies that he is an idealist at all:

> Idealism consists in the assertion that there are none but thinking beings, all other things which we think are perceived in intuition, being nothing but representations in the thinking beings, to which nothing external to them in fact corresponds. (288-89 in the Academy edition)

Distancing himself from such a view, Kant goes on to say,

> I, on the contrary, say that things as objects of our senses existing outside us are given, but we know nothing of what they may be in themselves, knowing only their appearances, that is, the representations which they cause in us by affecting our senses. Consequently I grant by all means that there

are bodies without us, that is, things which, though quite unknown to us as to what they are in themselves, we yet know by the representations which their influence on our sensibility procures us. These representations we call "bodies," a term signifying merely the appearance of the thing which is unknown to us, but not therefore less actual. Can this be termed idealism? It is the very contrary.

The resemblance of such a view to John Locke's representative realism is fairly obvious, and in this passage, unlike in the *Critique of Pure Reason*, Kant seems to welcome such a comparison:

> Long before Locke's time, but assuredly since him, it has been generally assumed and granted without detriment to the actual existence of external things that many of their predicates may be said to belong, not to the things in themselves, but to their appearances, and to have no proper existence outside our representation. Heat, color, and taste, for instance, are of this kind. Now, if I go farther and, for weighty reasons, rank as mere appearances the remaining qualities of bodies also, which are called primary—such as extension, place, and, in general, space, with all that which belongs to it (impenetrability or materiality, shape, etc.)—no one in the least can adduce the reason if its being inadmissible. As little as the man who admits colors not to be properties of the object in itself, but only as modifications of the sense of sight, should on that account be called an idealist, so little can my thesis be named idealistic merely because I find that more, nay all the properties which constitute the intuition of a body belong merely to its appearance.
>
> The existence of the thing that appears is thereby not destroyed, as in genuine idealism, but it is only shown that we cannot possibly know it by the senses as it is in itself. (289-90)

(Notice the phrase, "by the senses," in this last sentence. Does this suggest that perhaps some other mental faculty might succeed where the senses fail?)

Now if we had only Kant's perceptual idealism, as expressed in his *Inaugural Dissertation*, the Transcendental Aesthetic section of the first *Critique*, and these passages from the *Prolegomena*, Kant's philosophy would not have nearly the significance which it has. This sort of idealism, considered by itself, has close affinities to the views of a number of Kant's predecessors. In effect, Kant has simply taken Locke's doctrine of secondary qualities further than Locke himself takes it, so that *all* perceived qualities become as "secondary" as Locke's original secondary ones. Kant feels at this point, at least in the *Inaugural Dissertation*, that there are some qualities of objects which are not straightforwardly perceived but are rather apprehended by thought alone; such qualities include, presumably, existence, unity and plurality, and causation. These are qualities which can inhere in things in themselves (and subjects of experience in themselves), and it is by reflecting on such characteristics that the philosopher can engage in metaphysics.

This "eclectic" philosophy of Kant also bears considerable resemblance to the philosophy of Leibniz. It views each mind as a kind of monad, with no spatial or temporal relations to other minds or to anything else. If the mind depended upon perception alone, it would be trapped within its own individual consciousness, but by pure thought one may hope, to some extent at least, to penetrate the veil of space-time appearance and to have knowledge of things in themselves. It may also be said, finally, that Kant's philosophy at this stage bears a considerable similarity to that of Berkeley. In both cases there is a perceptual phenomenalism combined, inconsistently in Berkeley's case, with a sort of conceptual rationalism. (Berkeley's "rationalism" can be seen in his contention that in addition to our ideas, which, good empiricist that he is, Berkeley attributes solely to perception, the mind also has "notions" of itself and God, and that with these "notions" the mind can go beyond its own perceptual experience.)

During his "silent" decade of the 1770s, Kant developed his mature view of the nature of thought and its relation to perception in human experience. This doctrine of the understanding is the most profound and distinctively Kantian part of Kant's philosophy and represents a radical break with all previous thinkers. Kant believed, however, that he could take his insights about the conceptual component in experience and graft them on to the perceptual idealism which he had already developed. The two parts of his system do not fit together smoothly, however, and this is what creates the conflict between the kinds of idealism in Kant's philosophy.

Without getting into the details of Kant's account of judgment, we can remind ourselves that according to this doctrine all of the *thinkable, conceivable* aspects of anything represent features which the knowing mind "thinks into" its experience. Therefore these features, as well as the more obviously perceivable aspects of things such as their size, shape, and location in space and time, characterize the object of the mind's awareness only as this object appears, not as it is in its own intrinsic nature. These understanding-imposed features of the phenomenal world include, for Kant, unity, plurality, and totality, existence and nonexistence, substantiality, and causality.

Now one immediate implication of this doctrine is that the "mind" which, according to Kant, structures the phenomenal world by its imposition of this conceptual form, cannot be the individual human psyche. For as I have argued above (11-13), if existence, unity, plurality, and totality are phenomenal, mind-imposed characteristics along with space and time, then as individual persons you and I must obviously be parts of this phenomenal world. Therefore we, either individually or collectively, cannot be identified with the "mind" which creates this world through its cognitive activities. I have also argued (33-34) that if the individual you and I are thus brought down into Kant's phenomenal world, Kant will then be able to adopt the causal theory of perception, along with a distinction between primary and secondary qualities, as an empirical theory of the goings on within this world. Kant's theory of the activities of the understanding, therefore, although presented in a psychological idiom, cannot possibly be a story about individual human minds and their relations to the objects around them. When Kant introduces his theory of the understanding, his version of idealism moves away from the monadism of Leibniz toward a view of some all-encompassing Mind which thinks the world into existence. In this new form of idealism, Kant's philosophy is not located anywhere on a sliding scale from naive realism to Berkeleyan idealism at all. Kant could perfectly well be neutral with regard to *that* scale, for that scale represents an attempt to locate the individual human mind in its relation to the individual items of its awareness, and Kant's idealism based on the understanding cannot be a doctrine about the *human* mind at all.

Another fact about Kant's understanding-idealism is that in this doctrine the status of the thing in itself becomes very dubious indeed. Kant can no longer use the plural terminology in speaking of "things" in themselves, nor, for that matter, can he speak meaningfully of there being only *one* thing in itself. The thing in itself can no longer, as it does in Kant's sensibility idealism, have any sort of causal relation to the apprehending mind, "affecting" the mind to "produce" representations, since causality is itself imposed by the understanding and thus applies only within the phenomenal world. Indeed, since existence is a category of the understanding, Kant cannot even (as Schopenhauer points out) say that the thing in itself *exists*. Finally, since the notion of reality in Kant's doctrine of the understanding refers only to the categories and their applicability to sensory data, we must say that in this form of idealism the very contrast between reality and whatever is opposed to it (such as dreams, hallucinations, or even appearance) must obtain within the phenomenal, space-time world rather than between this world and something else. At this point it would seem that the thing in itself has been reduced to literally nothing at all. Why, then, should we hold on to this doctrine? Is it because only the "form" of experience is imposed by the mind, while the "matter" of experience must come from without? This may be true of the individual human mind, but why should it be true of the Mind which creates the phenomenal world? And if the cosmic Mind does not need a "given" upon which to direct its cognitively creative activities, there is then no need whatever for a thing in itself as a correlate to this ultimate Subject.

Chapter 6

"Empirical," "Transcendent," and "Transcendental"

A Modest Proposal

Some additional light may be shed on Kant's different forms of idealism by a consideration of Kant's use of the terms, "empirical," "transcendent," and "transcendental." I contend that although Kant does mean something very important by these terms when they are used to classify different kinds of knowledge, he departs from these original meanings when he speaks of empirical idealism and transcendental idealism. This is why these latter expressions, as Kant uses them in the first *Critique*, are of little use in understanding either Kant's philosophy or anyone else's.

Yet we need not jettison this terminology altogether. I will argue that we can construct better definitions of these expressions than the ones Kant provides. Given the Kantian meanings of the adjectives, "empirical" and "transcendental," I will propose an account of what Kant *ought* to have meant by "empirical idealism" and "transcendental idealism." In doing this, I will need to add a third expression to this already overburdened vocabulary, "transcendent idealism." My excuse for this highhanded way with Kant's terminology is my belief that my proposed definitions of "empirical idealism," "transcendent idealism," and "transcendental idealism" can tell us something about Kant's philosophy in ways in which Kant's own definitions do not. They will also, I hope, shed some additional light on Kant's inability to make his own form of idealism clear to his readers.

The adjectives, "empirical" and "transcendental," have their original home, in Kant's writings, in connection with knowledge. Empirical knowledge is knowledge about the observable, space-time world. Transcendental knowledge by contrast, is knowledge about knowledge. Kant, we remember, defines "transcendental" knowledge as: "all knowledge which is occupied not so much with objects as with our knowledge of objects in so far as this mode of knowledge is to be possible a priori" (A12). Actually, a more obvious contrast to empirical knowledge would be "transcendent" knowledge. This would be knowledge of "how things really are" beyond the world of our experience, the sort of knowledge which old fashioned metaphysics has always attempted to provide. Transcendental knowledge, of the sort which Kant gives us in the first *Critique*, adjudicates between the claims of empirical and transcendent knowledge. Once we have this transcendental knowledge *about* knowledge, once we see what knowledge essentially is and where a priori knowledge comes from, we will see that all the rest of "our" knowledge (if the "knowing subject" is the human person) must be empirical and that transcendent knowledge is not possible at all. Kant would say that prior to the discoveries in the first *Critique*, a philosopher might reasonably argue that any knowledge which was a priori in its origin must be transcendent in its scope. Transcendental knowledge, however, shows us that this a priori knowledge is an expression of the mind's own principles which it uses in structuring its experience and that therefore no knowledge which this structuring mind possesses, whether a priori or a posteriori, can reach any further than the phenomenal world which the mind creates by its intuition and thought.

Now if this is what Kant means by "transcendental," what should he mean by "transcendental idealism"? If transcendental knowledge is knowledge about knowledge, then transcendental idealism should be a doctrine which arises from such knowledge. Idealism is the theory that the mind in some sense determines or structures its object in knowing it, and so transcendental idealism should be an additional story to the effect that the mind must determine its object for there to be knowledge *of* an object at all, because this is what knowledge essentially is. Transcendental idealism would explain that knowledge requires the imposition of a "mental" framework upon the data of experience, that any knowledge therefore requires a basis of a priori knowledge, and that this a priori knowledge, because of its origin in the mind, can reach no further than the phenomenal world which this mind in some sense creates. All of this transcendental idealism is, of course, the story which Kant tells at great length in the *Critique of Pure Reason*. But transcendental idealism in this sense does not, for the reasons I have stated, provide any account of the

"Empirical," "Transcendent," and "Transcendental" 109

status ("empirically real and transcendentally ideal") of the space-time world and its relation to the individual human mind.

Is there a place for the expression, "empirical idealism," given Kant's meaning of "empirical"? Here again, if empirical knowledge is knowledge about the phenomenal world, then empirical idealism ought to be a doctrine about a mind which is itself part of this phenomenal world and is itself an object of experience. The best candidate for such a mind would be the individual human psyche. The finite human mind is, to some extent at least, part of the observable world, so any account of its operations in structuring its own individual experience would have to be regarded as empirical knowledge. This sort of knowledge would be gained at least in part through inner observation of one's own mind. The accounts of human mental operations which we find in the British philosophers of Kant's day, and especially in the writings of David Hume, would seem to fit this description and hence would merit the title of empirical idealism.

Transcendent idealism, finally, would have to be a kind of idealism that would be revealed to be true through transcendent knowledge. It would have to be the view that the space-time world is determined in its structure by a "mind" that is *not* the human psyche, is *not* part of the phenomenal world, and is *not* in any sense an object of experience. The "mind" of transcendent idealism would necessarily be something standing outside our space-time world as its necessary condition and holding in existence, among other things, the human minds that are a part of this world.

Now that we have distinguished these three forms of idealism, it would seem that transcendental idealism, as so defined, might be open to augmentation by some kind of empirical idealism. It could be so augmented only if the mind-imposed epistemic "form" is not as all encompassing as Kant makes it in his philosophy. If the perceptual and conceptual form includes as much as Kant wants it to include and if one insists, as Kant does, that all of this epistemic structure does *not* characterize either the object or the subject of experience as they are in themselves, then—as I have argued above—it is impossible to relate this form-imposing subject to human persons. But if transcendental idealism is defined in the noncommittal way in which I have defined it here, this sort of doctrine would allow the identification of the knowing subject with the human mind. And if such an identification were made, it would invite a further story about how the specifically human mind works in determining its experience.¹

Transcendent idealism, finally, is a doctrine that at least according to Kant, human beings should not try to entertain at all, because it requires the sort of transcendent knowledge Kant's transcendental discoveries have shown to be impossible for human beings. Even though transcendent idealism is a view toward which Kant is pushed by his doctrine of the understanding, and generally by his view that the necessary forms of experience characterize things only as they appear, it is something that is forbidden to human speculation by Kant's overall, transcendental view of the nature and limitations of knowledge.

A Disagreement With Allison

An important book by Henry Allison, *Kant's Transcendental Idealism*, contains an interpretation of the idealism in Kant's philosophy which is quite different from mine. Allison's interpretation of Kant is representative of a recent sympathetic trend in Kant scholarship which attempts to remove the air of paradox from Kant by interpreting his central doctrines in an "epistemological" rather than an "ontological" manner. Because Allison's view runs so far counter to mine, it should be considered here.

According to Allison, the only "mind" to which Kant is referring in his Copernican Revolution is the individual human psyche, yet Kant is in no danger of plunging into any sort of solipsism (or becoming, in Allison's phrase, "a Cartesian skeptic *malgré lui*"). This is because Kant, unlike most of his readers, distinguishes between the empirical and the transcendental versions of the contrasts between idealism and realism and between appearances and things in themselves. Considered empirically, the appearance/thing in itself contrast is between "the private data of an individual mind" and the "intersubjectively accessible, spatiotemporally ordered realm of objects of human experience." When Kant claims that he is an empirical realist, according to Allison, he is denying that a human person is imprisoned within his own individual consciousness and

---

¹This approach to a sort of transcendental-empirical version of idealism as an interpretation of Kant is represented in the recent "psychological" (in contrast to "epistemological") readings of the first *Critique*. See Zoeller, "Main Developments in Recent Scholarship on the *Critique of Pure Reason*," 457-61. The most persuasive advocate of such an approach today is Patricia Kitcher: see 28, above.

is affirming instead that our experience "includes an encounter with" a world which exists independent of our individual minds.²

The transcendental version of the distinction between appearances and things in themselves, according to Allison, is quite different from this empirical contrast. To explain Kant's transcendental move, Allison introduces the notion of an epistemic condition. This is described as a condition which "is necessary for the representation of an object or an objective state of affairs."³ It is in virtue of such conditions that human consciousness is able to relate to, or be an awareness of, an independent reality at all. Accepting Kant's distinction of perception and thought as distinguishable but equally necessary components of human experience, Allison claims that space and time are epistemically necessary conditions of the perceptual component of human experience, while substantiality, causality, and the rest of Kant's categories are conditions of its conceptual component. Put in another way, if the world of our awareness were not spatial and temporal, there could occur no human perception of it, and if this world, or the individual objects in it, were not substantial, causal, etc., then our minds could not make judgements about it and therefore could not conceptually relate to it.

Allison claims that this notion of an epistemic condition is "central to Kant's whole transcendental enterprise," and that such epistemic conditions must be distinguished both from psychological conditions and from ontological conditions.⁴ A psychological condition Allison characterizes as "some mechanism or aspect of the human cognitive apparatus" which is appealed to in explaining why human beings perceive or think about (or "experience") the world as they do. This can be understood to include physiological facts about the human brain or sense organs as well as "narrowly psychological factors" such as custom or habit as described by Hume or, presumably, any mental conditions or mechanisms which would be studied by modern cognitive psychology. An ontological condition is described by Allison as "a condition of the possibility of the being of things." It is a way in which any existing thing must be, in order to exist at all. According to Allison, Kant interprets Newtonian space and time as such intended ontological conditions and criticizes Newton for the

---

²Allison, *Kant's Transcendental Idealism*, 6-7.
³Ibid., 10.
⁴Ibid., 11-13.

dangerous theological implications of such a view: If space and time are necessary conditions for the *existence* of things, then they must be necessary conditions of the existence of God.

Kant's epistemic conditions, as Allison views them, must fall somewhere between psychological and ontological conditions. They are not ways in which objects in the world must *be*, nor are they ways in which the human mind (or any other mind) works in its awareness of these objects. Rather, they are ways in which the world must be *if* we humans are to have our "human" perceptual and conceptual apprehension of it. Kant does not claim, according to Allison, that these are conditions of *any* awareness of objects, only of *human* awareness. If the world were not spatial, temporal, substantial, etc., then we humans could not apprehend it, and any apprehension of a nonspatial, etc. world which did take place would not be a "human" awareness of it.

This notion of an epistemic condition enables Allison to explain Kant's transcendental distinction between appearances and things in themselves. Allison claims that this is an epistemological distinction between two ways of considering objects rather than an ontological distinction between kinds of things. In this transcendental way, to consider objects as appearances, or as they appear, is just to consider them along with those qualities which they must have if we are to perceive them or think about them, while considering these same objects "as they are in themselves" is simply to consider them apart from, or in abstraction from, these very qualities.

With this notion of an epistemic condition, and the "transcendental" distinction between appearances and things in themselves which follows from it, Allison then defines transcendental idealism as "a metaphilosophical or methodological 'standpoint,' rather than a straightforward metaphysical claim about the nature or ontological status of the objects of human cognition."[5] It is the standpoint which recognizes the existence and importance of epistemic conditions, as defined above, in human knowledge and which is thereby able to make the above mentioned "transcendental" distinction between appearances and things in themselves. Transcendental realism, which supposedly characterizes every philosophy prior to Kant's, is defined "negatively" as any philosophy which fails to "recognize the role of epistemic conditions in human

---

[5]Ibid., 25.

knowledge" and hence fails to make the transcendental distinction between appearance and the thing in itself.

The obvious question to ask about Allison's interpretation of Kant has to do with the status of these "conditions" which the mind "imposes" on its object. Does the mind in any way *cause* the object to be, or appear, in such a way as to conform to the mind's requirements for knowledge? Allison refers repeatedly to space, time, causality, and all the rest as 'subjective' conditions of human experience, and also calls them "a priori conditions which reflect the structure of the human cognitive apparatus." This latter characterization might suggest the standard picture of Kant, according to which the knowing mind is literally the source of space, time, and so on, so that these features all characterize what "we" are aware of only as it appears to us, not as it is in itself. Such a view seems to be expressed even more strongly by Allison's statement that for Kant, "whatever is necessary for the representation or experience of something as an object . . . must reflect the cognitive structure of the mind (its manner of representing) rather than the nature of the object as it is in itself."[6] To say that these features do not reflect "the nature of the object as it is in itself" would certainly seem to imply that the objects of human awareness are *not* spatial, temporal, and so on apart from their relation to human minds. We must remember, however, that for Allison the phrase "in itself," in the transcendental sense of this expression, just means "considered in abstraction from its epistemic conditions," from those features which an object must have if human beings are to have experience of it.

So what, if anything, is imposed by the human mind upon its objects? Allison tells us that according to Kant's "anthropocentric model" of knowledge, "the cognitive structure of the human mind is viewed as the source of certain conditions which must be met by anything that is to be represented as any object by such a mind."[7] Once we know what these conditions are, we may account for the mind's a priori knowledge of the objects of its experience, since "it is an analytic truth that any object represented must conform to the conditions under which it can alone be represented as an object." Therefore, all that the human mind "imposes" on its objects is the necessity that the objects must be a certain

---

[6]Ibid., 27.
[7]Ibid., 29.

way if humans are to apprehend them. This is all, according to Allison, that Kant's transcendental doctrine of epistemic conditions amounts to.

Allison's way of interpreting Kant's transcendental idealism certainly does take the philosophical sting and sense of paradox out of this doctrine. My objection to it is that it flies in the face of what Kant explicitly says and also runs counter to some of the central aims of Kant's philosophy. It also reduces some of Kant's most distinctive doctrines to triviality. Under Allison's interpretation, "appearances" or "things as they appear," in Kant's transcendental sense, just means *things*. These expressions refer to rocks, trees, planets, human bodies, human minds, electrons, and anything else which the universe may be found to contain. "Things in themselves" or "things as they are in themselves" refers to these very same objects, only this time considered apart from those features which they must have if we are to perceive them and think about them, i.e., if we are to "experience" them. The claim that things in themselves are nonspatial (and nontemporal, etc.) reduces to the claim that if we think about things in abstraction from their spatial (and temporal, etc.) features, we then find that these objects, *as so considered*, are nonspatial (and nontemporal, etc). Kant's doctrine of the limitation of human knowledge to experience becomes the platitude that we could not have knowledge of anything which did not have those characteristics, whatever they are, which an object must have if we are to have knowledge of it. The epistemic conditions which the human mind "imposes" on the world are like the ambulatory conditions which my legs impose upon a hillside—my legs "impose" upon the hillside the "necessity" of having a slope no greater than 40° if I am to be able to climb the hill.

Allison is at times rather hesitant about his own interpretation of Kant, admitting that if his interpretation is correct, there is "a great deal of misleading language on Kant's part,"[8] especially in Kant's repeated characterization of appearance as "representations only, which are one and all in us." And he admits that to rescue Kant from the apparent paradoxes of his idealism requires "a bit of help from the sympathetic interpreter."[9] The difficulty is to determine when this "bit of help" amounts to telling us what Kant ought to have said, rather than what he truly does

---

[8] Ibid., 59.
[9] Ibid., 3.

"Empirical," "Transcendent," and "Transcendental" 115

say or intends to say in his writings. There is nothing wrong with this latter project, but in this case one will have something like Strawson's or Bennett's picture of Kant, in which some of Kant's doctrines are explicitly modified or even deleted entirely in order to create a new "Kantian" philosophy more in line with present day philosophical tastes. I believe that this is what Allison has, in effect, done in his epistemological (rather than psychological or ontological) reading of Kant's idealism. In order to say that Allison's interpretation represents what Kant really intended to say, there is just too much of the text of the first *Critique* and the *Prolegomena* which must be treated with too much violence.

I have referred above to the psychological terminology which runs through the first *Critique* (29-30) and to the need to interpret Kant's Copernican Revolution in some sort of human-psychological sense in order to do justice to his claims regarding a priori knowledge and to his arguments in the Antinomies. But the Kantian doctrine which, I believe, tells most strongly against Allisons' interpretation is Kant's view of human freedom. Allison admits that in addition to practical freedom, which is the ability to act out of a conception of a rule rather than only in response to immediate sensuous impulses, Kant wishes to attribute to human beings what Allison calls transcendental freedom, which is the exception of human actions from causal necessity. Kant's way of doing this, of course, is to say that such necessity represents only "our" mind-imposed cognitive framework and therefore characterizes human actions only as they appear. But human persons and human actions as they are in themselves are *not* causally determined, and thus the reality of human freedom is not threatened by the inclusion of human beings *as they appear* within the space-time world.

Now let us see how this transcendental freedom appears under Allisons' interpretation. Considering a person according to his "empirical character," Allison says, is just to consider a person as part of the "phenomenal" space-time world. Since human beings *are* part of this world, this would seem to be a correct way of considering them. But Allison says that in order to conceive of a person as a free agent, we must consider this same person in his "intelligible character," which "turns out to be a much more complex and mysterious procedure." To form such a conception, we strip away in thought "all those features which pertain to its [the agent's] empirical character," including, presumably, the agent's causal relations to other objects and events. The result is, as Allison says, that "Since considered in this way the subject would not 'stand under any conditions of time,' it follows that we could no longer speak meaningfully of something happening in or to this subject, and thus of its being determined by antecedent conditions."[10]

In other words, "person in themselves are free" is analyzed similarly to "things in themselves are nonspatial": If you think about a person who (like all persons) is in fact subject to causal necessity, and if in thinking about this person you "consider" him apart from his causal determination, you will find that *as so "considered"* this person is not causally determined and hence is transcendentally free. This, I submit, reduces Kant's conception of human freedom to something of rather limited interest, and shows that a more robust interpretation of Kant's idealism than Allison's is required if we are to be true to Kant's own intentions.[11]

In his subsequent book, *Kant's Theory of Freedom*, Allison gives a much more extensive treatment of this topic, particularly regarding its relation to Kant's moral philosophy. In his interpretation of Kantian freedom itself, however, Allison holds to the position of his earlier work. He claims that the distinction between a person's empirical character (which is casually determined) and his intelligible character (which is free, meaning—among other things—that it is *not* causally determined) is only a distinction "between two 'points of view' or descriptions under which a single occurrence (a human action) can be considered."[12] To consider a person in his empirical character is to think of this person

---

[10] Ibid., 321.

[11] The "robust" interpretation of transcendental idealism, as against the purely epistemic interpretation which Allison develops, is argued for at some length in Paul Guyer's *Kant and the Claims of Knowledge*, 333-44. In the remainder of part 5—"Transcendental Idealism"—Guyer examines Kants arguments for transcendental idealism (interpreted robustly) and finds them wanting. But Guyer interprets transcendental idealism as simply the view that things in themselves are not in space or time and that spatiotemporality, and the schematized categorial determinations, therefore characterize objects only as they appear, etc. While I think this interpretation is correct as far as it goes, my claim is that to see the full incoherence of Kant's transcendental idealism, and the lack of any clear distinction between it and the empirical idealism with which Kant and some of his commentators wish to contrast it, we must ask my further questions about the status of the knowing subject and the relation of consciousness to its object.

[12] Henry Allison, *Kant's Theory of Freedom* (Cambridge: Cambridge University Press, 1990) 3-4.

"under the familiar belief-desire model" according to which a person is motivated, i.e. inwardly determined, by his desires, both short and long range, and his beliefs. To consider this same person in his intelligible character, by contrast, is to think of the person "transcendentally." So considered, the person possesses what Allison (and Kant) call freedom in the negative sense, which is simply exemption from causal necessity.

For Kant, of course, the most significant kind of human freedom is freedom in the positive sense, or spontaneity of the will, which Allison defines as, "the capacity to determine oneself to act on the basis of objective (intersubjectively valid) rational norms and, in light of these norms, to take (or reject) inclinations or desires as sufficient reasons for action."[13] In Allison's reading of Kant, it is our subjection to the moral law, revealed in our sense of moral obligation, which shows that we possess freedom in a positive sense; and this positive freedom, in turn, establishes the reality of freedom in the negative sense, although only "from a practical point of view."[14]

So are human beings in fact determined, in their decisions and behavior, by events in the space-time world, or are they exempt from determination by this causal sequence? Under Allison's "epistemic" interpretation of Kant, humans are in fact totally causally determined:

> Thus the claim is not that I only "appear" to myself and others as causally determined whereas I "really" am free. With respect to my empirical character, which encompasses everything that, strictly speaking, can be known about me as a rational agent, I really am causally determined, just as I really am a spatiotemporal being. This is just the force of Kant's empirical realism.[15]

What, then, is the purpose of "considering" human beings in any other way than as they truly are? If space, time, and causality (etc.) are for Kant "epistemic" rather than "ontological" conditions of objects, that is, if these are features which objects must have if they are to be perceived and conceived (i.e. "known") by us and are not (for all that we can tell) conditions of the very being or existence of any objects whatever, then their status as only "epistemic" conditions opens up a "'conceptual space' for the nonempirical thought (though not knowledge) of objects,

---

[13] Ibid., 5.
[14] Ibid. Allison develops this argument in chap. 13 (230-49).
[15] Ibid., 44.

including rational agents, as they may be apart from these conditions, that is, as they may be 'in themselves'."[16] Allison's use of quote marks in his reference to objects "in themselves" reminds us that "in themselves" does not mean "as they truly are in their own nature," but rather only "considered apart from certain features which they in fact have," in this case causal determination.

It is difficult to see, under this interpretation of transcendental idealism, how Kant could suppose that this view of things protects morality and freedom from the findings or presuppositions of empirical science. If Kantian freedom is just causally determined human behavior with the determinism abstracted (or "considered") out of it, it is not obvious what interest we should have in such a doctrine. And if our sense of moral obligation forces us to think that (or "as if") we are truly exempt from causal determination, then such a belief and the sense of duty which gives rise to it should be regarded as fictions in the Humean sense—things which we are perhaps psychologically forced to accept but which we have no reason to believe characterize the real world.

What Kant intends to say, I believe, is not simply that causal determinism can be "thought out" of human agency if we choose to think it out, or even that we are forced to so think of ourselves when we are aware of moral obligation. He is saying rather that causal necessity is thought *into* human behavior, and everything else in the phenomenal world, by the knowing mind, so that (contra Allison) human beings are not "really" causally determined in their own nature but only "appear" to act under causal necessity because of the conceptual activities of the observing and thinking subject. This interpretation of transcendental idealism will open up much more than just a "conceptual space," in Allison's sense, for human freedom; and only such a robust view of human freedom and of the transcendental idealism which makes it possible will do justice to what Kant wants to say about the ability of human beings to act as moral agents.

If we ask whether the idealism in Kant's philosophy, is to be interpreted in an epistemological, or psychological, or ontological manner, my reply is that it should be interpreted in all of these ways. Kant is indeed concerned with the nature and possible scope of human knowledge. He sees such knowledge as having the two components of

---

[16]Ibid., 44.

perception and thought, and he is certainly concerned to find the necessary conditions in human experience for the operation of each of these components and therefore for knowledge as a whole. But as Strawson points out, whenever Kant finds what he considers a necessary condition of experience, he explains its necessity by putting the source of this feature itself (i.e., the source of space itself, not just the source of the *necessity* of objects being spatial if we are to perceive them) within the mind. This is clear, I think, from the text and from certain Kantian doctrines such as that of human freedom. But this psychologizing move has ontological implications, since it makes for a real, not just a methodological, distinction between objects as they appear and these same things as they are in themselves. And as soon as Kant has made his psychological move, with its ontological consequences, the questions about the exact status of this knowing mind and its relation both to individual human minds and to the "external" objects of its experience become pressing ones.

There is one final objection which can be lodged against Allison's interpretation. Kant's aim, according to Allison, is to find the epistemic rather than the psychological or ontological conditions of human knowledge. These conditions are to be discovered not by an examination of the human mind or human mental activities (this is the job of cognitive psychology) nor by an ontological enquiry into the overall nature of the universe. They are to be discovered, presumably, by a conceptual analysis of our ideas of knowledge and experience. But of course Kant is not trying to find the necessary conditions of experience per se, but of "our" experience, that is, human experience. Much of the burden of analysis will therefore shift over to the meaning of "human." The task will be, I suppose, to simply think hard about what we mean by expressions such as "human knowledge" and "human experience" in order to come up with analytic truths about how the world must be if human experience of it is to occur. Apart from the meager prospects for success in such an undertaking, there is the question of how one could maintain an airtight separation between it and the empirical enquiries of the cognitive psychologist. For the concept "human" is an empirical one, and so surely our concept of *human* knowledge or experience and its necessary conditions will be affected to some extent by what scientists can tell us about how the human mind works in its cognitive operations. It would seem, therefore, that as long as Allison, and Kant, are concerned with *human* knowledge, they will not be able to keep their researches as separate from empirical, psychological enquiries as they would like. (We have seen that Patricia Kitcher takes Kant's philosophy in precisely this direction. See above, 28.)

Mention should be made here of an important recent article by Kenneth F. Rogerson which puts forward an alternate, and more extreme, version of the "epistemic" interpretation of transcendental idealism.[17] Like Allison, with whose interpretation Rogerson compares his own, Rogerson interprets the Kantian subject as "imposing" nothing more upon the world than the requirement that this world be spatial, temporal, and causal in order to be knowable by human beings:

> Ordinary objects of experience are "mind-dependent" only in the sense that for anything to count as an object about which we can give true or false descriptions it must fulfill our ("mind-imposed") epistemic requirements.[18]

Rogerson goes beyond Allison, however, in suggesting that these features are requirements for any reality to be, in any way, an object of human thought. He refers to some of the passages in the Transcendental Deduction which I have discussed above in relation to Kant's coherence or necessary-connection theory of objective reference (69-77); these parts of the *Critique* do indeed convey the view that "real," for any knowing subject, implies "in principle knowable," so that the very idea of an inherently unknowable reality must be meaningless. But Rogerson's interpretation of transcendental idealism as a " 'nonreductive,' semantic, antirealism" requires him to downplay or ignore entirely Kant's transcendental psychology with its talk of the subject literally creating or at least structuring the objects of its experience. Rogerson also, unlike Allison, does not deal at all with Kant's treatment of freedom or with the Antinomies generally. Furthermore, he does not recognize the correspondence theory of truth which, I contend, is to be found in the *Critique* along with the coherence view. He therefore has no use for a substantive conception of the thing in itself and he admits that if his own epistemic interpretation of transcendental idealism is accepted, much of what Kant says about the thing in itself must be jettisoned.

Rogerson's article provides an interesting Kantian perspective upon the debates between realists and antirealists in present day epistemology.

---

[17]Kenneth F. Rogerson, "Kantian Ontology," *Kantstudien* 84:1 (1993): 3-24.
[18]Ibid., 20

But his need to ignore some important Kantian doctrines and to downplay others shows that his "semantic" version of transcendental idealism cannot stand as a convincing interpretation of what Kant truly intended in his philosophy, or even as a plausible reading of Kant which is supported by the text of the first *Critique*. Rogerson's interpretation represents rather a drastic alteration of Kant's philosophy in order to make it more plausible and more relevant to present day debates. His efforts lend support, I believe, to my contention that if we take *all* of Kant's doctrines seriously, there is no single view of the mind's relation to its object which we can call Kant's transcendental idealism.

Chapter 7

Epilogue.
Kant without Idealism?

We may now consider whether Kant might be liberated from the idealist elements of his thought, and whether such a revised Kantian philosophy might present an answer to Cartesian scepticism. Given the ways in which idealism in various forms is bound up with Kant's philosophy, the prospects for success in such an undertaking appear dim.

First of all, in any version of Kant's philosophy which is to be taken seriously by present day philosophers, at least in the analytic tradition, the subject of experience must be the individual human person. Also, if the subject is the particular you and I, we must adopt some sort of relational or correspondence view of the outward reference of consciousness. We have seen from Wolff the difficulties which one gets into if the self is the individual person and the relation of consciousness to its object is just the unity of this consciousness itself. Such a view results in a physical world which is real only in a Pickwickean sense and it allows no sense at all to an individual's thought about other subjects of experience. To allow for other minds and to allow as well for their genuine embodiment as human persons, we must have a space-time world which is independent at least of individual human (and animal) subjects of experience. And because these are the only kinds of subject which we have any reason to believe exist, it is doubtful to what extent the resulting view could justifiably be called idealist. As long as I and the physical world which I apprehend are two different things, we might accept any one of a large number of accounts about this world as it appears to me versus the same world as it is in itself; but the existence of the physical world as a material, space-time order which exists independently of the conscious beings which inhabit it, must be accepted as ontologically ultimate.

Can we extract any such view from Kant? To see the prospects for doing this, let us consider again how Kant regards his project in the Transcendental Deduction of the Categories. We can get a fairly clear picture of what Kant is attempting in the Deduction by considering Kant's own explanation of the title of this section. To "deduce" a concept, Kant says, is to give a justification for its use. It is to show that this concept applies to the world, such that the use of this concept can give us knowledge of how things really are. Most of our concepts would be capable only of what Kant would call an empirical deduction, which would be a matter of simply pointing to something in the world to which the concept applied. Only empirical concepts, those which require some specific sensory data for their use, would be capable of such a justification. For certain other concepts, however, this kind of justification would not be possible. Our concepts of substance and cause, for example, do not seem to be tied to any specific sensory data and so could not be "deduced" in any straightforward, empirical way. As Hume has pointed out, as far as simply our idea of cause is concerned, anything may cause anything. Hume's conclusion is that our concept of cause is not "justified" in that its central idea of force or necessity is a fiction of the imagination to which nothing out in the world corresponds. Berkeley had, of course, earlier come to the same conclusion about the idea of material substance.

For these concepts and others Kant wishes to give a transcendental deduction. This will consist in showing that experience would be impossible without the use of these concepts. And by their use Kant must mean their valid use in something far beyond the Humean sense. Kant would not be satisfied with any explanation to the effect that the mind is forced, through whatever internal causes, to make use of conceptual "fictions" which tell us nothing of how the world which we perceive and think about really is. Kant's deduction will consist in showing that the use of these concepts which experience requires is one which gives us knowledge of the world which we experience.

It is well known (among Kant scholars) that in spite of the title of the Transcendental Deduction of the Categories, Kant does not here attempt to "deduce" or even discuss in any detail any of the individual categories. This is not attempted until the Analytic of Principles. So what is Kant doing in the Transcendental Deduction? If my proposal is correct that Kant's concept of the transcendental object or "object in general = X" can be equated with our concept of "real world" or "how things are" or "object of our awareness and knowledge per se," then the Transcendental Deduction can be seen as an elaborate deduction of this concept. Here Kant's project must be seen in its historical context as an attempt to answer Descartes's central question in the *Meditations*. Kant is trying to justify or deduce the concept of objective reality by showing Descartes that his idea of a real world which is the object of his consciousness is not a fiction but is valid, that his consciousness must in fact be an awareness of a real world. (After showing this, Kant will go on to show some of the features which this real world must necessarily have, given that it exists in time.) It is the attempt to show the *validity* of "real world" and the concepts which are included within it which marks off Kant's project most sharply from that of Hume.

So how does one show the validity of the concept of "object of consciousness per se?" It would seem, initially at least, that one does this by showing that consciousness is essentially relational. Descartes begins with the view of consciousness as a monadic property, the essential attribute of a spiritual substance. But viewing it as simply a characteristic of "I," Descartes asks how each of us can know that there are any other objects and attributes in existence aside from his own "I" and its consciousness. In Descartes and other thinkers we find an inferential argument in which a physical world, or God, or something else external to the mind is posited as the only, or most likely, cause of consciousness. Kant, however, wants no part of such an approach. He does not wish to show that consciousness is caused by an object but rather that it is "of" an object in a more essential way than this. He wants to show that once one has consciousness or experience, one already *has* "the object," and this can only be to show that consciousness in its very nature *includes* both subject and object.

How, more precisely, does Kant do this? Here we must draw on another part of the historical context, namely Hume's puzzlement about the self. In his *Treatise of Human Nature*, having shown to his own satisfaction that there is no reason to believe in a persisting substance, spiritual or otherwise, in which states of mind inhere, Hume then wonders what it can be which makes different "perceptions" part of the same conscious experience (book 1, part IV, section 6). Does Kant, like Hume, regard this idea of the connection among conscious states as something problematic and in need of explanation? To answer this question, one would be helped by knowing more about the extent of Kant's familiarity with the writings of Hume. Patricia Kitcher argues convincingly, against Kemp Smith, that Kant knew about Hume's attacks on the self through the writings of Beattie and others and that he intended his own work to be a response to Hume's view of self-awareness and personal identity as well as to Hume's theory of causation.[1] Yet it is hard to know the degree to which Hume's arguments motivated or influenced Kant on these matters, because in all of Kant's deliberations on self-consciousness in the first *Critique*, he never mentions Hume or, as far as I can tell, even refers to him indirectly. This is particularly striking in the Paralogisms, where Kant argues repeatedly that my awareness that all of *my* representations are *mine* does not involve any additional intuition, and that therefore there is nothing in my self-awareness for any concept to apply to, whether this concept be that of a spiritual substance or anything else. This is in agreement with Hume's failure to find within himself a persisting ego, so if Kant had been influenced by Hume on this point we might expect to find some mention of it, especially in view of Kant's willingness to acknowledge his debt to Hume on other matters.

Whether or not Kant consciously intended his writing on self-awareness to be a reply to Hume, could we regard it as such? Could we say that Kant is implicitly attempting with his doctrine of judgment to answer both Hume and Descartes at once by showing the logical connection between the unity of representations in a single consciousness and the status of this consciousness as being "of" a real world? We could argue that Kant's major philosophical tools for this purpose are his distinction between intuitions and concepts and his theory about what concepts are and what function they perform in experience. With this theory of judgment, perhaps, Kant attempts to make two initially problematic notions clear and to show their relation to one another. For of course, if *both* "unity of consciousness" and "awareness of an object" are obscure, little will be gained by merely analyzing one of these ideas in terms of the other. Some third, comprehensible doctrine will be needed to connect them. But does Kant's theory of judgment tell us what these expressions really mean and thereby enable us to answer the questions of both Descartes and Hume?

Kant scholars who have addressed themselves to this question have alternated between attempts at pure exegesis, staying close to the text and telling us how Kant himself intended his argument to go, and "recon-

---

[1] Kitcher, *Kant's Transcendental Psychology*, 97-102.

structed versions" of Kant's argument in which the commentator in effect constructs his own argument out of Kantian materials. I can only say that I cannot see that any Kantian argument, either in Kant himself or in his commentators, has fully answered either Descartes on the external world or Hume on personal identity. We may admit Kant's contention that judgment, which is thinking or mentally "asserting" that something is the case, goes beyond the mere having of sensory data before the mind. It is a kind of mental activity which we may perhaps describe as combining or putting things together, and this is furthermore the act by which the subject "says how things are" and thus refers outside of himself to an external reality. These are crucial Kantian insights which have changed many of the very terms in which epistemological questions since Kant have been posed. But do they answer Descartes and Hume?

They do not answer Hume because surely not all of the items in my consciousness, two pains at different times, for example, can be said to be part of the same mind or same consciousness through being connected together in judgments. Such items are usually not "connected together" in any sort of judgment at all, even though each is included within my consciousness. Perhaps we should not criticize Kant for this failure, however, since he may not have been addressing himself to Hume's labyrinth about personal identity. But does he answer Descartes? Does he succeed in reassuring the doubtful Cartesian that there is in fact a real world with which his consciousness puts him in touch? Here again, we must answer that he does not. Kant's deepest and most considered view of the relation of consciousness to its object is his coherence theory, according to which this relation to an object is nothing more than a necessary connection among the parts of consciousness themselves. If the subject of this consciousness is taken to be the individual human being, this theory will imply a solipsism which will hardly be reassuring to the Cartesian.

But could Kant's argument be altered so as to prove that the consciousness of an individual person is, or logically requires, a genuine *relation* between this person and an ontologically independent reality? The prognosis for this is poor. We have seen that where Kant adopts a correspondence view of consciousness, he simply assumes the existence of an independent object rather than arguing for it. All of the actual arguments about the relation of consciousness to its object are bound up with the coherence theory. In connection with this doctrine, we could certainly argue in Kantian fashion that my making of judgments, this conceptual activity which I perform upon my sensory data, is what gives me a sense of an objective reality which my consciousness is directed toward. It also, perhaps, gives me a sense of myself as the subject of this consciousness and as something different from the external world which I apprehend. Sensory data alone, whether caused from without or from within, would not be enough to give to the subject the idea that this awareness was "of" any object at all, nor would this sensory "matter" give to the subject any idea of himself as having or receiving it. All of this is maintained by Strawson in *The Bounds of Sense*.[2] But as Barry Stroud points out in his article, "Transcendental Arguments," these arguments are not sufficient to answer the skeptic about the external world.[3] For the skeptic could say that this shows only that for experience to be possible the subject must *believe* that his consciousness is an awareness of an external reality. But what guarantees that this belief is true? After all, surely in dreams there are sensory data which are subjected to some sort of conceptualization or recognition process. If a dream can occur for any time at all and if a dream is an occurrence of consciousness which is not an awareness of any real, existing object, then there would seem to be nothing logically incoherent in the proposal that this may occur more often and for longer periods than we think, or even that there might exist a creature whose entire conscious experience was one continuous dream. To flesh out this possibility we could bring in the well-worn hypothesis of the mad neurophysiologist, the modern equivalent of Descartes's evil demon.

An attempt to refute this sort of skepticism about the external world is made by T. E. Wilkerson.[4] In a passage of his commentary which looks very much like a defense of Strawson's "reconstructed version" of Kant against Stroud's criticism, Wilkerson asks whether the necessary application of concepts of objectively real things proves that this is a correct or valid application. He replies that although in most cases it does make sense to distinguish between the successful and mistaken application of a concept, we cannot use such a distinction to entertain coherently the possibility of "complete and perpetual illusion" regarding the existence of a physical world independent of consciousness:

---

[2]Strawson, *Bounds of Sense*, 97-110.
[3]Barry Stroud, "Transcendental Arguments," *Journal of Philosophy* 65 (1968): 241-56.
[4]T. E. Wilkerson, *Kant's Critique of Pure Reason* (London: Oxford University Press, 1976) 58-59.

Epilogue. Kant without Idealism?

To make any distinction we must have a way of drawing the distinction. . . . But if all perceptions were illusory we would not be able to say so, for we would have no way in experience of telling the difference between perceptual success and perceptual failure. . . . In a state of complete perceptual illusion we would have no way of distinguishing between perceptual failure and perceptual success, or more generally between merely applying concepts of external things and successfully applying them. But to have no way of drawing a distinction is to have no distinction. Thus, once we have proved that we must apply concepts of objects . . . we have in effect proved the existence of the external world.

I am afraid that this will not do as a refutation of the sceptic because it begs the question at issue. The sceptic such as Hume argues that in fact we *cannot* (successfully) tell the difference between the correct and mistaken application of our concept of "reality external to my consciousness." Hume argues that there is a difference between certain of our perceptions and certain others in vividness and internal coherence and that we mistake this difference for a difference in real external reference. In his *Treatise* Hume has an elaborate story to tell about how this mistake is made, about how we mistakenly suppose that we are directly, noninferentially aware of independently existing objects (book 1, part IV, section 2). Perhaps Hume's account is wrong, but to show that this scepticism is incoherent surely requires something stronger than Wilkerson's argument. And bringing in Kant at this point, rather than any "reconstructed version" of Kant, would be a mistake because according to Kant the coherence or connectedness of certain of my perceptions just *is* their reference to an external reality. This doctrine would not be pleasing to either Strawson or Wilkerson because it runs quite contrary to the relational view of consciousness which they would like to extract from Kant.

Yet we should admit that in spite of the different directions in Kant's thought, the deepest part of Kant's philosophy contains an idealism which is too robust to be easily used by present day philosophers. Kant maintains in his doctrine of concepts that reality itself is a construction of the mind and that the reference to a real external world is something which the mind thinks into its own consciousness. If we accepted such a view as true, our only hope for avoiding solipsism would be to go in the direction of later Idealist thinkers and to say that this creative mind is not the individual human being but rather something which can encompass individual persons plus the rest of the universe in its consciousness. But even if such a doctrine could be made plausible, we would still have the question of how each of us human beings can be sure that he is not dreaming, now or perpetually.

Perhaps this sceptical hypothesis, however presented, is in fact impossible. Perhaps my individual consciousness could not be simply an objectless dream that puts me in touch with no reality outside of this consciousness itself. My contention here is only that the impossibility of this is not shown by anything which Kant says about intuition and judgment as necessary components of experience, or by any of the forms of idealism which result from this distinction. We must admit, therefore, that the prospects are dim for using Kant's philosophy as an answer either to Hume's uncertainty about the unity of consciousness or to Descartes's doubt about the external world.

Index

Adickes, Erich, 15, 18-19
Allison, Henry, vii, 1-2, 4, 49, 68, 95, 110-20
Ameriks, Karl, viii, 2, 41, 60
Antinomy of Pure Reason, 8-9, 15-17, 26, 48, 53, 87, 115
Austin, John, 62

Barker, S. F., 50-51
Beattie, James, 126
Berkeley, George, 5, 7-9, 19, 23-24, 32-33, 38-40, 43, 48, 53, 56, 58, 68, 78, 93, 104-105, 124
Bennett, Jonathan, 28, 59, 65
Bird, Graham, 48-49

Copernican Revolution in Philosophy, 15, 29, 43, 64, 110

Descartes, René, 7-9, 20, 45-46, 52, 61, 66, 69, 72, 78, 82, 85, 90, 92-93, 96-97, 123, 125-28, 130

Findley, J. N., 1
Freedom, 16-17, 26, 115-18

Guyer, Paul, vii, 90, 116

Hume, David, 45, 60-61, 70, 80, 109, 118, 124-27, 129-30

Inaugural Dissertation, 73, 102-103

Kemp Smith, Norman, 2, 19-21, 27, 34, 37, 39, 53, 65, 75, 98, 126
Kitcher, Patricia, 28, 110, 125-26

Leibniz, Wilhelm Gottfried, vii, 11-13, 22, 24, 59, 73, 104-105
Locke, John, 5-9, 14, 33-35, 37, 39-40, 50, 52, 59, 103

Metaphysical Deduction, 29-30

Nagel, Thomas, 63
Neoplatonism, 5
Newton, Isaac, 39, 111-12

Paralogisms, 6, 9, 30-31, 37, 39-41, 75, 89, 91, 126
Paton, H. J., 2, 23-25, 32, 50, 53, 65, 95-96
Prolegomena, 9, 11, 40, 43, 48, 88, 102-103, 115

Refutation of Idealism, 26, 39-40, 88-93
Rogerson, Kenneth F., 120-21

Schrader, George, 21, 30, 98
Schopenhauer, Arthur, 53, 105
Straud, Barry, 128
Strawson, P. F., 1-2, 4, 25-28, 31, 43, 47, 49, 53, 63-67, 78, 81-82, 95-96, 119, 128-29

Turbayne, Colin, 7, 68

Walker, Ralph C. S., 27
Wilkerson, T. E., 128
Wilson, Margaret, viii, 45, 68
Wolff, Robert Paul, 53, 73-74, 92, 95-98, 123

Vaihinger, Hans, 102

Zoeller, Guenter, 95

Kant's Idealism.
by Philip J. Neujahr.

Mercer University Press, Macon, Georgia 31210-3960.
Isbn 0-86554-476-X. Catalog and warehouse pick number: MUP/P122.
Cover and text and interior designs, composition, and layout by Edd Rowell.
Camera-ready pages composed on a Gateway 2000 via WordPerfect
 dos wp/5.1 and wpwin/5.1/5.2, and printed on a LaserMaster 1000.
Text font: TimesNewRoman PS.
Display font: (heads) Arial (TT); (cover titles) DTC Mistral
Printed and bound by Braun-Brumfield Inc., Ann Arbor MI 48106.
 Printed via offset lithography on 60# Natural Smooth paper.
 Perfectbound in 10-pt. cls stock, printed one PMS color
  (Pantone 504c = 13/3/4 Warm Red, Reflex Blue, black + 10% screen),
   and film laminated.

[May/June 1995]

GENERAL THEOLOGICAL SEMINARY
NEW YORK